The Paradox of Plenty

Existential Strategies for Decisive Living

Casper Brix

ISBN: 978-87-974188-3-3 (print)
ISBN: 978-87-974188-4-0(ebook)

CONTENTS

Part 1: Introduction 7

Preface 9

A Greater meaning.......................................13

What the book aims to achieve............................15

Part 2: The dilemma of choices 19

An abundance of options.................................21

"Whatever..." 29

The (never-ending) pursuit of something better 35

Part 3: An introduction to existentialist philosophy...........45

Existentialist philosophy.................................47

The different philosophers 51

What the philosophy offers you...........................65

Part 4: The problem with choosing 71

The value of our choices.................................73

Irrational decisions 81

To compare your choices.................................93

One's true self 105

Being happy and having choices 109

Part 5: The weight of our choices 115

The happiest country in the world 117

Finding happiness in our actions 135

What about the next generation? 147

Part 6: Existentialist philosophy in practice 149

How to use existentialist philosophy 151

Existentialist perspectives 155

Sisyphus smiled up the mountain 205

Make a difference—for yourself and others

PART 1: INTRODUCTION

"The crucial thing is to find a truth which is truth for me"
–Søren Kierkegaard[1]

---

1   From the original Danish quote: "Det gjælder om at finde en Sandhed, som er Sandhed for mig, at finde den Idee, for hvilken jeg vil leve og døe". Søren Kierkegaard (Gilleleje, 1835)

PREFACE

Do you also find yourself buying the same items every time you visit the supermarket? And do you feel, at the same time, that your choices are somehow being made by others, even though everyone tells you the world is at your feet? Likely, only a few of us reflect on how we make decisions—and what impact our handling of these choices has on our well-being. In this book, I will offer you an insight into how you can apply research into consumer behavior along with existentialist philosophy to gain a deeper understanding of the opportunities and choices that make sense specifically for you.

In our modern society, numerous options are constantly presented to us. This could be, for instance, when we are in the supermarket trying to decide what to buy for dinner, or when we face larger decisions, like which education to pursue, which career to chase, whom to vote for in the next parliamentary election, what kind of love life we desire, or how we want to raise our children. Everywhere we turn, we encounter opportunities that require us to make decisions and take action.

The average person in a Westernized country today lives with several options that would have seemed unattainable to someone growing up just 30 years ago. Back then, neither the internet nor globalized trade existed, which could offer the same opportunities as they do today. On the contrary, many people in these societies now live where they want to and seem not to be significantly limited by material goods. They choose what they want to eat, what clothes they want to wear, whom they marry, where they want to work, what they want to watch on TV, and increasingly, where in the world they want to settle.

The freedom to choose should have a positive effect on our mental well-being, but in fact, the latest figures from the Danish Mental Health Fund (2021) show that this is perhaps not the case. Instead, our mental well-being has seen a negative trend, which is also reflected in the estimate that about one in three people in Denmark is expected to develop a mental illness at some point in their lives. With an outset in such statistics from Denmark and abroad, you will discover the correlation between the number of our options and the increased pressure it puts on each of us as individuals.

The opportunity to choose is a privilege, and therefore there should be no doubt that our choices contribute to improving our lives. We have the option to buy organic coffee from Ethiopia, the finest argan oil from Morocco, and Kobe beef from Japan. Our options make it possible in many ways to piece together exactly the life we want to live. However, these many options also entail a number of challenges, and if you ask leading researchers in psychology and modern consumer behavior, it is not necessarily good that we have as many options as we do.

Drawing on research, this book will help to illustrate why we should reflect on how we respond to the opportunities presented to us. As you will come to understand, it is possible to have too many options, which can lead to negative consequences, because as humans, we do not want to reject things in life; on the contrary, we want to choose as much as possible.

As our welfare increases, we also experience more freedom—a freedom that creates opportunities. Opportunities that require us to make choices. However, these choices also place a responsibility on the individual, and this can negatively impact whether we feel satisfied and happy with our lives. In this book, I aim to show, on a research-based foundation, the connection between our happiness and the increasing number of options we face every day. By combining recent studies focused on the complications our choices bring and the existential philosophical approach to living life through our actions, I will attempt to pave a way to make life—and its many opportunities—less complicated.

In the book, you will find examples of how existential philosophy can act as a healthy reality check in managing the large number of options you are constantly presented with. For me, a philosophical approach to life has played a significant role. It helps me gain perspective on my own actions and find peace in the choices I make. Instead of constantly doubting whether something is right or wrong, I would rather accept that nothing should be different and that everything is as it should be. This is an approach that existential philosophers describe with the term *amor fati*, a love of fate, and the ability to see all experiences in life as inherently positive.

In a world full of choices and alternatives, it assists me in pausing to appreciate where I am and what I have, rather than dwelling on where I am not and what I lack. The aim is to focus on how I want to live, rather than how others think I should. Therefore, when I catch myself pondering what others believe I should do, or over things I cannot influence, I can use existential philosophy to refocus on myself. Through this, philosophy aids me in changing my understanding of my options and the choices I make. I tell myself that I do not need to work, but I can choose to. I do not need to attend a social event, but I can opt to. I do not need to study in a specific program, but I can decide to do so. Thus, I remind myself that I should not view my options as a series of choices to satisfy others, but rather to satisfy myself.

At first glance, the freedom spoken of by existentialists seems like an additional burden on all of us modern individuals who are constantly faced with a multitude of choices. However, if you delve deeper into their ideas, as we will do in this book, you will discover that existentialist philosophy assists you in accepting that it is better to just make a choice, rather than to remain passive in the hope that a better alternative will present itself. But they also tell us that this requires you to focus on your own choices based on your own authentic needs—not others'. As you will learn, the philosophy helps you to recognize and accept that you cannot choose objectively 'right', but you must practice appreciating the choices you make because they are your own.

Only when we manage to view our actions from a distance does it become possible to assess whether we are making them based on our own needs, or whether the overwhelming weight of our options causes us to place the responsibility for our actions on others. I hope that this book will show you that it is okay to feel overwhelmed by the many opportunities that our welfare and freedom bring. And that it does not mean you are neglecting the value of your freedom. On the contrary, I also hope that this book will help you understand that we live in a time with an unprecedented number of options. Therefore, we must step back and evaluate which opportunities we wish to seize—and what creates value for our own lives.

A GREATER MEANING

The fact that you have started reading a book like this suggests that you are questioning what it means to live a fulfilling life. Like most of us, you probably also wish to live the best and most meaningful life possible. However, there is no instruction manual telling you how to be happy. On the contrary, you have to figure it out by yourself, which can create a sense of anxiety. As you are aware, in the end, the responsibility for your own actions is left in your hands.

These are precisely the thoughts on which existentialist philosophy is based. As an individual, you exist with the desire to find a greater meaning in your life, but you also know that this meaning will not arise on its own. The philosophy helps to convey that you must create meaning from your life and existence. The modern society is full of options, which, in the existentialist understanding of life, can often be seen as distractions. These distractions shape you on your journey towards your goals. At the same time, in modern society, you may also encounter challenges and losses, all of which can make you doubt whether there is any greater meaning at all. All these concerns are thoughts that existentialist philosophy addresses, making it well-suited to assist us in examining the complications that our options entail.

The original thoughts of existential philosophy stem from Denmark, where Søren Kierkegaard helped lay the foundation. His well-known words, "life must be understood backwards, but it must be lived forwards",[2] illustrate existential philosophy's focus on our actions. Moreover, this philosophy underscores the idea that we have to live our lives as they happen, since we cannot plan them in advance. We are condemned to only be able to understand life in the clear light of hindsight, despite our desire to see into the future and know which actions would be the best to take. Unfortunately, we will never know the answer, for the answer lies only in the past, as Kierkegaard explains. According to existentialist thought, your life only becomes meaningful when you choose to give it meaning. This process occurs through your actions and interactions with your surroundings. In an era where our options may seem overwhelming, this philosophical direction offers to cut through all distractions and focus on what truly matters.

In alignment with existentialist thought, this book is not a manual. You may choose to understand and use the content of the book in many different ways, as no one but you can know what brings value to your life. Existentialist philosophy points out the way to reflect on the world in a manner that enables you to take your own independent path among life's many options. It invites you to ponder why you are here and where you want to go, as your life is not static but something you can influence and define.

Or as Friedrich Nietzsche, another important philosopher within existential philosophy, said: "Become who you are."[3]

---

2   Kierkegaard, S. (2009). *Frygt og bæven.*

3   Nietzsche, F. W. (2015). *Schopenhauer som opdrager.*

WHAT THE BOOK
AIMS TO ACHIEVE

Before you read on, I want to elaborate on what this book aims to achieve—and what it does not aim to achieve. The primary purpose of the book is to help you put your actions into perspective. Therefore, it is not intended as a self-help guide. As mentioned, this idea goes against the existentialist understanding of what it means to live a meaningful life.

Instead, the book can lead you to reflect on the choices you make in a way that makes sense. In a complex world full of options, this is perhaps more important than ever before.

The book does not offer a 10-step plan to make you happy. However, I hope that you will take action on the reflections it encourages. It is up to you. But, as you will see in the following, according to existentialist thought, your actions are what constitute your life. The question is not whether you need to make decisions to live a meaningful life or not. No, the question is how you make the right decisions in relation to how you want to see yourself, rather than how you want others to see you.

With this purpose in mind, in the book's introduction, I will start by reviewing a series of the most important scientific studies on how we, as humans, make our decisions. Then, I will explain the main thoughts of existentialist philosophy (hereafter just called "the philosophy") and introduce four of its most important thinkers. This book only provides an introduction to existential philosophy, as the goal is not to provide a complete explanation about all of its details. The focus is instead on the perspectives on today's multitude of choices that it can create for each individual. Based on this, you can then choose how you want to use the philosophy to help navigate you in your day-to-day choices.

Throughout the book, I will present various issues that may have arisen in connection with the many opportunities of modern society.

These problems are contrasted with results from relevant studies on consumer behavior and perspectives from a range of different existentialist philosophers. A combination of consumer research and philosophical knowledge allows you to form a diverse understanding of the topic.

It is important to clarify that I myself do not have a formal education in psychology or philosophy. My background is in marketing, where I have been fascinated by why we as humans do what we do. I am intrigued by studies on how humans act in decision-making processes, which often originate in consumer behavior. There has been long-standing research into how to get people to buy a specific product or service. But these same studies can also be used to reflect on what generally drives us to make decisions, or, in relation to this book, what leads us to choose some options over others.

Thus, this book should be seen as a bridge between some of the most groundbreaking studies on how we, as humans, respond to opportunities (consumer behavior) and the existentialist understanding of how actions define our lives.

As you turn to the next pages, you will read about the dilemma of choices. Why is it called a dilemma? Well, several studies seem to have found a correlation between an increased number of options (and thus the number of decisions we need to make) and the rising number of people affected by mental disorders such as anxiety, depression, and stress. When something positive seems to affect us negatively, it can be said it is dilemma. A rather paradoxical dilemma, you might say.

Then, you will be introduced to some of the main figures in existentialist philosophy. Finally, you will get an overview of the complications that our numerous options are believed to cause, and how they can affect our happiness and contentment. And in the end, the book once again addresses existential philosophy—this time to present the movement's more concrete perspectives, which should make us better at making decisions based on our own desires.

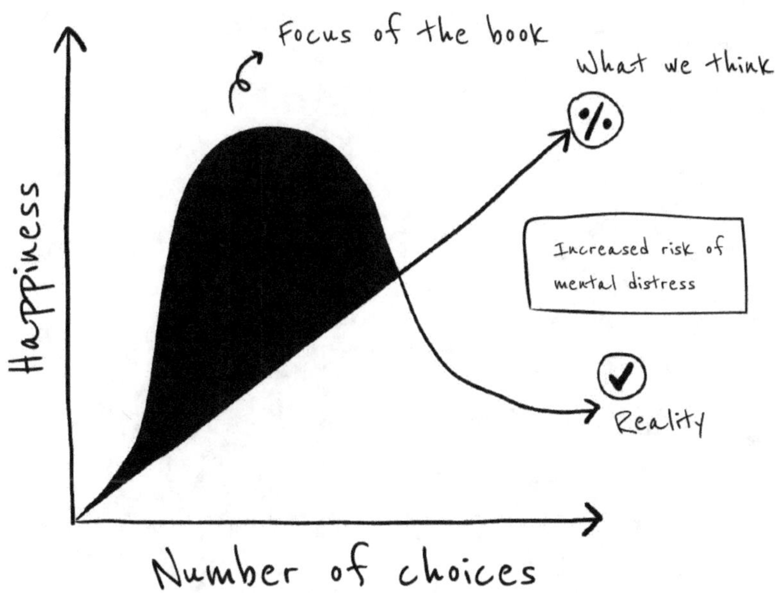

PART 2:
THE DILEMMA OF CHOICES

"Everything has been figured out, except how to live."
–Jean-Paul Sartre

AN ABUNDANCE OF OPTIONS

For many years, we have focused on creating more opportunities in the Western world. The goal has been to create as many options as possible for everyone, so that each of us can live precisely the life we desire. This pursuit of welfare and freedom has granted us more options today than ever before. However, alongside the privilege of our freedom and the right to choose, we also find ourselves faced with an unprecedented number of decisions to make.

In our quest for more options, we seem to have forgotten how to handle them.

More opportunities have been created for the individual. Previously, choices were limited to a few alternatives, making it less complicated to make the most advantageous decision. Yet, this task has become more complicated as we have moved from evaluating what seems good and bad to, instead, assessing what is better and best. From a societal perspective, this is tremendously good news, but from an individual perspective, a different picture emerges.

More options mean more alternatives, all requiring us to make choices and decisions, which can lead to a series of paradoxical complications. On one hand, one is free to choose; on the other hand, it simultaneously becomes more difficult to choose. It is a development that appears to continue, emphasizing the growing importance of making well-informed decisions.

But what are the consequences of our many options, and how do we ensure that we make the right choices?

In the next part of the book, you will gain insight into how we, as humans, react when options are presented and choices are needed to be made. Before we can grasp the connection between the multitude of choices we face and our mental well-being—which is an essential goal in itself—it is crucial to first comprehend the fundamental mechanisms that underpin our decision-making process.

Our options

In modern society, we have more options, seemingly driven by the understanding that more is always best. As consumers, this becomes apparent when we walk into the local supermarket. Here, we encounter rows filled with various types of everyday items: 10 different kinds of dishwashing liquid, 20 different brands of toilet paper, and 30 types of different bags of chips. But it is not just in the supermarket where we face the challenge of choosing and rejecting the things we want. We also do this when it comes to our careers, love lives, and personal finances.

According to a study from Cornell (2007), we make an average of 221 decisions daily about one thing: what we eat. This number has likely grown since. Everywhere we go, we are faced with options. As will be discussed in the following section, it seems to influence a large part of the way we choose to live our lives. Most of us probably grew up with the mindset that we should have everything "our way". That we should have the opportunity to customize everything so that it perfectly fits our needs. That it will make us happier. But that might not always be the case.

Let's try a simple thought experiment. You have gone on your dream trip to Italy with your partner, and after a long day filled with great experiences, you decide to find some delicious local food. So, you start hunting for the right restaurant, but after a while, you have to give up the search, as all places are fully booked. Therefore, you choose to sit at one of the more touristy restaurants, as by this point, you are quite hungry—and the familiar bad mood associated with low blood sugar on a city trip is slowly starting to spread. You sit down, but to your great surprise, you are presented with a menu of over 200 different dishes. Everything from Chinese, Thai, Mexican—you name it. You do find a few Italian dishes, but it does not make the choice any easier. You both end up ordering a dish you already know, even though it has nothing to do with the local cuisine. You both feel overwhelmed by the choices, and at this point, you are too hungry to consider all 200 dishes, so you choose something familiar. Finally, you make the safe choice, falling on a tasteless sandwich for you and a bland burger for your partner. After the visit, you tell yourselves that it may not have been the experience you had hoped for, but at least you got some food.

Do you also know the feeling of having to settle for a tourist restaurant that is just okay, even though you could have picked something better? Or the moment of giving up when faced with a massive menu, only to order a dish you already know? It is a familiar scenario for many. However, it is rare for us to realize that we encounter similar situations regularly with the abundance of choices in our everyday life. And it is even rarer for us to consider that we often react in the same way, whether a 200-item menu is presented to us or we are shopping for groceries in our local supermarket.

As the next section will show, this is a normal reaction and is all about how our brains deal with an increasing number of options. What is more interesting, in terms of our society, is that the range of our choices has never been larger.

Therefore, we are also at a greater risk of feeling this same sense of resignation, whether we are at an average restaurant in Italy or facing an important decision that will impact our lives.

A restlessness in our actions

Before, there was only one type of mobile phone, a few educational paths, and a single local pizzeria. Today, the options are almost endless. This means we have to make more and more decisions. Which course of study should we choose? Where do we want to work? Who do we want to spend our time with? Additionally, we also have to ensure we choose the right partner, the right clothes, the right food, and so on.

And we must do this while constantly telling ourselves to be in a good mood and grateful, because we have so many options. Our expectations of ourselves and our choices of actions are incredibly high, thus increasing the pressure on ourselves to choose the best options we encounter.

To live, we must make decisions. There is no escape, as our existence is intertwined with action. But, as will be described, it appears that the more options we are presented with, the worse we become at choosing.

Our ability to choose is linked to the idea of being free, but as the book will show, too many options can create psychological imbalance. As already explained, our multitude of options can lead to a fear of making the wrong decisions. As the number of options grows, so does this fear, creating a restlessness about the actions we take. In this way, we come to associate our options with fear, which manifests in our behavior.

Below are some of the thoughts that influence how you handle your options. These points stem from the research you will read more about in the upcoming sections of the book, where each will be discussed in more detail.

Thoughts that influence how you handle your options

We are missing out on more and more: The multitude of options makes us realize that we are missing out on more and more. We simply cannot grasp everything that life offers us. Just as we are about to start a new series on Netflix, doubts arise about if it is truly the series we most want to watch. We know that starting a new series means we cannot watch another at the same time. We say yes to one thing, and, thus, no to another. The fear provoked by what we miss out on when we grab one opportunity over another is immense, as we are constantly reminded of all that we are losing.

We have higher expectations: When more options are made available to us, we also build higher expectations for ourselves. Due to increasing welfare and greater access to resources from all over the world, we are constantly reminded of the things we lack. Moreover, we compare ourselves more with others, which reminds us of all that we are not. As a result, we create higher expectations for ourselves, which can have negative consequences for our well-being and understanding of the world.

We want a bit of everything: We have become accustomed to the fact that we can have more and more, and therefore we also seem to want more and more. It is in our human nature to acquire as much as possible in an attempt to survive, but our biological nature also stops us from letting go and focusing on all that we have. Instead, we choose to focus on all that we do not have by trying to get a bit of everything. We forget to pause and remind ourselves that if we only get a little bit of everything, we never really get anything.

We get used to the way things are: Over time, we adapt to our surroundings. Eventually, to such an extent that we no longer notice that we are doing it. All our choices (or lack thereof) become normal—just as everyone else's choices also become normal. Therefore, when we come to think about the many choices we could have made instead, it creates anxiety, because we are made aware that there is a different life contrary to the one which we are already living.

We blame ourselves: Every time we make a mistake, we are quick to blame ourselves. We forget that failing is healthy and a natural part of growing as a person. Instead, we blame ourselves for not being able to fully utilize life. We also forget that it is inevitable to fail—especially when life demands more and more actions. It creates a sense of guilt because we think we owe ourselves the best. Thus, the many options constantly remind us that we could do better, which leads us to blame ourselves.

We compare ourselves to everyone else: As it becomes harder and harder for us to make our own decisions, we start looking at others. We watch what others do—and do not do—while we seek acceptance from our surroundings that can confirm the choice we have made. Unfortunately, it also leads us to forget to make our own decisions, as we would rather seek security among others. Our life becomes less authentic because we are constantly trying to compare ourselves with others.

We tell ourselves that nothing is good enough: Imagine you have finally found the right series on Netflix to binge-watch all Sunday. You have even found the perfect take-away to satisfy your hunger after carefully studying menus from 10 different restaurants. You think your Sunday is saved. But, unfortunately, it is only for a short while. The dilemma induced by our abundance of choices still makes you think that nothing is ever good enough. The series is good, and the food tastes nice, but what if the other series you were considering, or the other takeaway place, had been better? Whether it is a Sunday on the couch, our work, our love life, or something else entirely, we increasingly live with the perception that it can always be better. But this feeling only does more harm than good, as it provokes anxiety and possibly apathy in individuals.

The points above are based on the research that underpins this book and will be presented in the following sections. But do these studies of principles—in connection with the opportunities and choices of life—have anything to do with you? Yes, more than you might think.

"WHATEVER..."

Have you ever faced a situation so complex that you ended up thinking, "Whatever... Does it even matter?" It is a sentiment many of us encounter at some point, a mental shrug in response to overwhelming complexity.

The sheer number of choices and the consequential decisions can be daunting, often leading to a sense of anxiety. This arises from having to determine which options to pursue amidst the inherent risks each choice carries.

As the frequency of decision-making escalates, so does the possibility of making the wrong choice.

In response, we often push ourselves to work harder to avoid mistakes. Yet, striving for a mistake-free life, driven by the fear of failure, is virtually unachievable. Deep down, we recognize this reality. Facing a maze of complex choices without a clear win in sight can strip us of direction. Without this, life begins to feel aimless. When we reach this point of complexity and start thinking "Whatever..." our actions risk becoming meaningless. We shy away from making firm decisions and instead look to others for cues. This leads to a weakening of our authenticity and a gradual loss of our sense of purpose.

In a study by Sheena Iyengar and Mark Lepper from Columbia and Stanford University (2000), researchers explored how people react to varying amounts of choices. They conducted an experiment that had a significant impact on modern marketing. On one day, they set up a stand with 24 different types of jam; on another, only six. The aim was to observe how the quantity of options affected consumer behavior.

While the stand with more jam varieties attracted more attention, it resulted in fewer purchases. Conversely, the stand with just six types of jam led to up to ten times more sales.

Their findings indicated that too many choices could lead to decision paralysis. Overwhelmed by the array of options, many people opted not to make any choice at all. Additionally, consumers from the stand with more choices reported feeling less satisfied, burdened by the thought that they might have missed a better option. This concern often showed as regret over not choosing a different flavor, like blackcurrant instead of the strawberry they selected.

The experiment also showed that when people were faced with a wide range of options, they often chose what they were already familiar with. For instance, they might pick the strawberry jam over the blackcurrant simply because they knew how strawberry jam tasted like. The study indicated that a vast array of choices could cause consumers to rely on their "automatic brain" to minimize the potential regret of a poor decision. Thus, an abundance of options did not just negatively impact sales but also the level of motivation and satisfaction among the participants. This study has been replicated across various industries and beyond the food market context, consistently revealing that:

an excess of options negatively affects our perception of a given situation. Evidence suggests that more is not always better, especially not in the realm of modern consumer behavior.

Building on the findings from the jam experiment, researchers delved into the psychology of choice, examining why we favor certain selections over others. As shown in the jam experiment, a limited selection resulted in more sales and greater customer satisfaction. But the underlying cause was more complex than initially thought. The researchers pinpointed three primary reasons why consumers might choose a specific product when faced with a multitude of options:[4]

> 1) The ability to make a quick and easy decision
> 2) Difficulty in comparing it with alternative solutions
> 3) Being made aware of what they really wanted

Let's start with the first motive, which is particularly interesting when talking about the overabundance of choices for modern individuals. Why? Because we are more inclined to make a specific choice if it seems easier than the other options we are introduced to. Even though most of us know that the easy and quick choice is not always the best.

It speaks to our increasing tendency to spend a lot of time on social media, rather than doing something more constructive like reading a book or cleaning the house. There is even a term for your procrastination, called 'instant gratification'.

This is what keeps you on social media instead of vacuuming the house, continuing your study project, or working. And there is a good reason for it. According to the latest report from the Danish Ministry of Culture (2021), 90% of the Danish population has a profile on one or more social media platforms. The report also shows that, on average, Danes spend nearly four hours per week on social media, with higher figures among young people. We seem to

---

4   Chernev, A., Böckenholt, U., & Goodman, J. (2015) *Choice overload: A conceptual review and meta-analysis*

have a craving for quick and easy choices, and this is partly reflected in our use of social media.

Looking at the second motive, it shows that we feel more drawn to a specific choice if we find it harder to compare it with other options. In the jam experiment, this was evident as fewer options created more sales and greater customer satisfaction. We find it easier to commit to a particular decision if we do not have to compare it with too many others.

The last motive that the study revealed is that, as consumers, we do not always know what we want. Steve Jobs once said, "People don't know what they want until you show it to them." Maybe there is some truth to it? Maybe we all want to be reminded of what we might like instead of having to decide for ourselves. Looking at modern consumer behavior, we do not have to look far for a possible reason for this. We are bombarded with advertisements and impressions everywhere, all telling us what we need to live a perfect life.

There seems to be a correlation between the way we perceive the options we are presented with and the way we react as consumers. If we feel we have too many options, we have trouble choosing. We seem to associate our options with a particular value, which makes us believe that we can eventually lose value if we choose incorrectly. At the same time, the increasing number of options leads us to seek easy decisions, either by letting others make us aware of what we want or by choosing based on previous experience. If we have made the decision before, it does not seem as daunting.

Losing faith in our ability to choose

Can we lose faith in our ability to make choices? In a study by Martin Seligman (1972), it was found that we can teach ourselves to believe we have no control. We can actually learn to become helpless when making decisions, a concept he defines as 'learned helplessness'.

In one of his studies, he conducted a two-part experiment involving three groups of animals and a task to jump over a small barrier to avoid a mild electric shock. In the first part, the first group of animals received shocks but could stop them by pressing a button. The second group also received shocks but could not stop them, even if they pressed the button, hence they had no control over being shocked. The third group served as a control and neither received shocks nor had to press a button.

In the second part, all animals were placed in a closed area with a small barrier in the middle. Staying on one side meant receiving shocks, but crossing over to the other side meant avoiding them. The aim was to see how the first part of the experiment would affect their ability to avoid shocks. The first group, having already been exposed to the shock but learned they could stop it, quickly jumped over the barrier upon feeling the shock in the second part. However, the second group behaved strikingly differently. Seligman expected this group to also jump over the barrier, but surprisingly, all the animals in the group became completely passive. Because of their experience in the first part, they believed they had no choice but to be shocked. Therefore, they did not try to avoid the shock by moving around or jumping over the barrier. They did not attempt to escape either; instead, they became passive and lay down until the experiment was stopped.

From this experiment, Seligman concluded that the animals in the second group had learned that they could not change the outcome and avoid being shocked. They had essentially learned to be helpless. In contrast, the first group learned that they could influence the outcome and avoid the shock. Instead of lying down, this group jumped over the barrier and quickly learned they could avoid the shock by staying on the other side. They could act and make a decision because they saw they had the option to do so.[5]

---

5   Seligman, M. E. P. (1972). *Learned Helplessness.*

Our options are tied to the belief that we can make our own choices. But as the experiment demonstrates, we can also teach ourselves to become helpless and convince ourselves that we have no options. If we learn to see ourselves as helpless, it can have serious consequences. Primarily, it can lead us to believe we have no control when faced with new situations. It can also affect the body's immune system and make us more susceptible to illnesses, as well as lead to depression. Research has shown that our ability to be in control of our actions—and avoid learning to be helpless—is closely linked to our sense of happiness and well-being.[6]

Is it possible that the sheer number of options we face puts us at risk of becoming helpless? Are we in danger of losing faith in our ability to choose simply because there are too many options? And if so, how do we then make our decisions? It seems that when we lose faith in our ability to choose for ourselves, we are more likely to place the responsibility on others rather than on ourselves.

**We may not be able to control the options
presented to us, but we can control how we react
to them, and, importantly, how we choose
among them.**

---

6   Seligman, M. E. P. (1975). *Helplessness: On Depression, Development, and Death.*

THE (NEVER-ENDING) PURSUIT
OF SOMETHING BETTER

As we age, we gradually come to realize that we cannot do everything. We start to understand that our decisions involve saying yes to some aspects of life and letting go of others. We learn that our choices come with a cost—the opportunities we decide not to pursue.

American psychologist and author Barry Schwartz (2004) has explored how our approach to choices seems to have divided people into *choosers* and *pickers*. Choosers engage in rational thinking and may take a significant amount of time to consider before making a decision, aiming to identify the most optimal choice. Pickers, on the other hand, tend to rely more on their intuition and are content with a decision that seems good enough.

For example, if two individuals, one a chooser and the other a picker, were to buy new shoes, their methods would be quite different. A chooser would find it challenging to simply go to the nearest mall and select from the first few pairs of shoes that fit in style and comfort. Instead, this person would invest time in exploring all available options to ensure they pick the perfect shoes. It would not be surprising for a chooser to spend days gathering all the necessary information on the best possible pair. In contrast, pickers would spend much less time deciding. They do not feel the need to evaluate all pros and cons and can make a quick decision. They would be satisfied with a pair of shoes that seems good enough, without needing to confirm that they are the absolute best option.

Herbert Simon (1947) was one of the first to describe this split in human decision-making with his concept of *satisficing*. Satisficing means choosing the first option that meets a satisfactory level, rather than continuously searching for the best one. As a Nobel Prize-winning economist and psychologist, Simon suggested that this approach could save both time and mental energy. He believed that the principle of satisficing could be applied across various aspects of life, especially in how we make decisions.[7]

Similarly, the concept of *analysis paralysis* syndrome explains how an abundance of options can render us incapable of making decisions. This occurs when we overthink a problem by weighing all its pros and cons.[8] And by overthinking our decision-making process, we risk creating unnaturally high expectations for the choices we make. In developing this concept, it has also been shown that people are more likely to regret their decisions if they spend an excessive amount of time making them.[9] Consequently, the shoes that our chooser eventually selects are more likely to bring less satisfaction, even though the person spent more time finding them compared to our picker.

The question then arises: is there a risk of creating an imbalanced society when our choices are based on the belief that there is always something better out there? Imagine a generation reluctant to settle down with a partner and get married, constantly thinking that a better partner might be just around the corner. Studies have shown that spending a lot of time weighing the pros and cons when

---

7   Simon, H. A. (1947). *Administrative Behavior: A Study of Decision Making Processes in Administrative Organization.*

8   Kurien, R., Paila, A. & Nagendra, A. (2014). *Application of Paralysis Analysis Syndrome in Customer Decision Making.*

9   Crosier, B. & Donahue, K. (2009). *Buyer's remorse: A personal and revealing look into what we want and why we shouldn't.*

choosing potential partners online can negatively impact people's ability to find a partner.[10] Our inclination to keep all doors open is also evident in modern individuals' career choices, where it has become commonplace to change jobs every two or three years. Figures from recruitment companies show that 26% believe they will switch jobs within three years, while statistics from Denmark reveal that young people aged 25-29 tend to change jobs on average after just two years.[11] [12]

So, what keeps us clinging to the idea that something better is out there? What drives us to shy away from a simpler life as our world becomes more complicated? Perhaps we can find answers in the way we assign value to the choices we make? People who place a great emphasis on making the right decisions build up a fear of failure. They set high standards for themselves, but as described, this also increases the likelihood that they will be disappointed with their choices. Humans have a remarkable imagination that aids us in being creative and thinking outside the box. We can not help but imagine what our lives would look like if we had seized one opportunity over another. We cling to thoughts of how happy we might have been if we had chosen to live elsewhere, chosen a different career path, a different partner, and so on. But these are distractions from the life and realities we actually have and the choices we can make.

When we act without thought

Consider this example: Are you someone who enjoys taking photos with a DSLR camera? Maybe you are familiar with the feeling of using the manual settings of your camera for better control, rather than relying on its automatic function. The manual setting allows

---

10   Yang, M. & Chiou, W. B. (2010). *Looking online for the best romantic partner reduces decision quality: The moderating role of choice-making strategies.*

11   AS3 (2021). *AS3 Jobsurvey 2021.*

12   Djøf (2021).

you to edit the photos in the right format, even though it takes longer to take the pictures. With the automatic setting of the camera, it is easier and quicker to take photos, but you cannot edit them in the same way, resulting in lower quality.

The way you choose to take photos serves as a fine analogy for how each of us makes decisions. We can either follow a set of automatic settings that make things a bit easier but do not ensure the highest quality results. Or, we can use manual settings to be part of the entire process, likely leading to better outcomes. The former requires the least investment but also results in poorer photos. Our automatic actions lead to less optimal decisions.

According to research in consumer behavior, we often switch between automatic and manual actions when making decisions. However, few of us are aware of when we do one or the other. In 1999, Baba Shiv and Alexander Fedorikhin conducted a thought-provoking experiment that demonstrated this. In their experiment, they asked two different groups to remember a number and then walk through a corridor to tell the number to a person at the end. Half of the participants were given a two-digit number, while the other half were given a seven-digit number. One group was presented with a more challenging task as they had to remember more digits.

Here is where the experiment gets intriguing. The researchers placed two different snacks in the hallway that the test participants had to walk through. They were instructed to choose either a piece of fruit or a piece of chocolate cake. The experiment revealed that of the individuals tasked with remembering seven digits, 63% chose the cake while only 41% did when they had to remember just two digits. Those with the more demanding task were more prone to succumb to their immediate inclinations. After facing a challenging cognitive task, they let their intuition take over, leading to actions based on automatic behavior patterns. Overwhelmed with the task of remembering seven digits, they automatically chose the cake. In contrast, participants who only had to remember two digits were not subjected to the same mental strain, allowing them to think more long-term and thus more likely to choose the healthier option. The conclusion drawn from the experiment was that thoughtless actions, in an automatic behavior pattern, lead us to make more mistakes. The way to avoid these mistakes is by not overloading our mental energy level, which is used for decision-making. This can be applied to modern society, where the overabundance of decisions strains our mental energy. We feel compelled to consider everything presented to us, weakening our ability to think clearly in our interest (manually). Instead, we fall back on acting without further consideration of the consequences of our actions (automatically).

If our daily life is characterized by having to make many decisions, we tend to react without considering what our actions entail. We end up in a state of *analysis paralysis*, overwhelmed by options and choices. Maybe you recognize this after a long workday filled with decisions, yet you still have to remember to do grocery shopping on the way home. Perhaps you do not venture into cook a new dish for dinner, even though you saw an exciting cooking show on TV last night. There is a greater chance you will shop for a meal you already know because your depleted mental energy level drives you to rely on your routines, your automatic behavior pattern. But what if you were in that state all the time—not just in the supermarket on your way home from work? What if all the choices you need to make leave you in a constant state of analysis paralysis?

The various experiments demonstrate how decisions can drain our mental energy reserves and affect the choices we make. There appears to be a correlation between the number of decisions and their quality. Studies have shown, for example, that medical clinic staff are more likely to make errors later in the day. Why? Because after a day filled with many decisions, they have depleted their energy reserves, which impacts the choices they make.

Similar studies have been conducted with judges. It was found that they are more likely to deny parole later in the day. Why? Because their energy level is lower after making decisions on numerous cases, making it seem like an easier and safer decision to deny parole.[13]

The term "decision fatigue" explains how the number of decisions we make contributes to exhaustion and leads us to make poorer choices. Described as a syndrome which most people experience on a daily basis, decision fatigue sets in as the day progresses and we reach our limit of decision-making capacity. Just as our muscles tire from exercise and use, our brains also grow weary from processing a multitude of choices and options.

Every day, all individuals are faced with numerous decisions to make, and none are spared from the fatigue that accompanies them. So, when you find yourself buying the same ingredients for dinner (again), it is likely because you are experiencing decision fatigue. After a long day, you have used up your daily "quota" of decisions, and your mental energy is depleted. But there is a valid reason for feeling tired. According to a Wall Street Journal article from 2015, we make an average of 35,000 decisions every single day, a figure that has possibly increased since then. With that in mind, it is understandable if you feel exhausted after a long day.[14]

When our energy is depleted, we are more likely to revert to bad habits and procrastination, or we may let others make decisions for us. It seems we can reach a point where our mental energy reserves are empty, creating room for decisions that require less effort. These typically manifest as procrastination activities; like watching TV, letting others make decisions for us, or spending the evening scrolling through social media on the couch. Essentially, these are actions that do not add value to our lives but also do

---

13   Danziger, S., Levav, J. & Avnaim-Pesso, L. (2011). *Extraneous factors in judicial decisions.*

14   Sollisch, J. (2016). *The Cure for Decision Fatigue: Choosing not to make choices might be the best response to the daily avalanche of options.*

not demand any effort from us. However, this can have significant consequences if we are not mindful of the number of decisions that we make unconsciously, as it can lead to postponing valuable tasks.

But as you will see in this book, there are several things you can be aware of to avoid getting caught up in endless procrastination and to understand why people behave as they do. In the end, you and your brain function like the doctor's and the judge's at the end of a long day. Just as their decision-making is influenced, so is yours.[15]

Adapting to change

Consider how our lives have evolved over recent years. Our consumption patterns have led to the emergence of entirely new needs which we have never had before. And with these new needs, we have also created a lack of clarity in our lives.

The options are endless, and we want a bit of everything. Maybe you, like me, also have 10 pairs of shoes at home because you think you need different choices for every occasion. Or perhaps you have several types of jackets to cover all seasons and weather conditions. One for rain, one for exercise, one for going out, one for everyday use, and so on. And then there is that jacket you impulsively bought and rarely use but still do not want to part with. Many of us would struggle to remember when we had just one item for each purpose. It seems that our needs have changed. Not just in terms of our clothing but also our general needs in life.

As we become wealthier and have more options available, our focus has shifted from securing food and survival to self-actualization. In Abraham Maslow's renowned work "A Theory of Human Motivation" (1943), he described how human needs constantly evolve as our basic needs are met. As soon as we satisfy these, we gradually move towards self-actualization in an effort to find mean-

---

15   Vohs, K., Baumeister, R. & Twenge, J. (2005). *Decision Fatigue Exhausts Self-Regulatory Resources—But So Does Accommodating to Unchosen Alternatives.*

ing in our lives. As of now, despite the supply crisis, inflation, and energy crisis, it does not seem like we will lack any essential needs in the foreseeable future in our part of the world. In many parts of the world, the trend towards greater material wealth will continue.

In his book "Utopia for Realists" (2017), Dutch author Rutger Bregman suggests that future crises will not manifest in a lack of material goods. Instead, he believes they will unfold in humanity's ability to find and create meaning in life. All basic needs will be met, leaving us to find meaning in our lives on our own. Whether one believes Bregman's prognosis for the future is a matter of personal perspective. But one thing is certain:

**our options do not seem to be diminishing.
This leaves us with no choice but to learn how to
handle the downside of them.**

The abundance of options, in many ways, leads to greater pressure on our expectations. We see what others have, and we want the same. With all these choices, we are reluctant to settle for what merely seems "good enough." The increasing focus of society on freedom and self-actualization, combined with many options, also leads to setting unrealistic goals for ourselves. We tell ourselves that we should be independent, beautiful, intelligent, caring, and successful—all at once. These thoughts are not meant as a critique of our freedom and options but as an encouragement to learn how to handle the privilege that our freedom affords us. As a society, we have achieved what previous generations could only dream of: an open and accessible world where we can realize almost anything we desire. But it comes at a cost: among other things, there seems to be a growing anxiety in our society about being insignificant, a fear of being just like everyone else.

When we no longer have to struggle for survival, we choose to fight to stand out. By standing out, we feel that we are realizing our potential, and our existence. How we, as humans, choose to do this will be illuminated in the next part of the book, where I will use existentialist philosophy.

PART 3:
AN INTRODUCTION TO EXISTENTIALIST PHILOSOPHY

"You are free and that is why you are lost"
–Franz Kafka

EXISTENTIALIST PHILOSOPHY

Existentialist philosophy is defined as a philosophical and literary movement focusing on the individual's freedom to choose and the accompanying responsibility of shaping one's own life. This school of thought has been influenced by various philosophers over time. Although each philosopher has their own understanding of life, they all advocate, in their own ways, for human freedom and the responsibility that comes with it.

Existentialism posits that humans are not born with a predetermined destiny; rather, we are capable of creating our own. Embracing this freedom requires courage. The philosophy highlights the uncertainty and anxiety inherent in life but also explains how through action and self-awareness, we can find meaning. Existentialism serves as a branch of the broader existentialist philosophy. However, this book takes the liberty of discussing existentialist philosophy as a unified movement, interchangeably referred to also as existentialism, rather than delving into its multiple branches. This is done to communicate its messages more clearly, and not focusing on its various branches and differences.

There are many clichés associated with existentialism, but a brief introduction is helpful to clarify its core principles.

Existentialism gained prominence after World War II, with Jean-Paul Sartre, Simone de Beauvoir, and Albert Camus playing key roles in popularizing the movement. Their extravagant lifestyles in Paris, characterized by open relationships and lively jazz club parties, became somewhat symbolic of existentialist philosophy. This portrayal has had mixed effects: it helped spread important existentialist themes but also contributed to enduring stereotypes. This image has sometimes hindered the philosophy's contemporary relevance. However, its roots extend beyond Paris, tracing back to the 19th-century Danish philosopher Søren Kierkegaard, who laid the groundwork for the movement.

At its core, existentialist philosophy focuses on the individual's quest to find meaning in their existence. The term 'existential crisis' is often used in everyday speech, referring to a state that goes beyond mere discomfort, touching upon deeper emotional struggles.

Kierkegaard's phrase "truth is subjective" encapsulates a key existentialist idea: everything starts with the individual. The philosophy posits that each person holds their own truth about life. Your beliefs are uniquely yours, distinct from others'. Likewise, what brings happiness or sorrow is personal and varies from one individual to another. What affects you may not impact another in the same way, as it all depends on how you relate to your environment and experiences.

You might experience being fired from your job as an existential crisis, causing you immense pain. However, this pain is subjective, as it is based on your own understanding of the value you attribute to your work. Another person might not perceive being fired as an existential crisis if they do not have the same emotional attachment to their job.

Death is another significant theme in existentialism. According to this philosophy, you have only one life, and no matter how long it lasts, it will be brief in the grand scheme of the universe. This understanding serves as a motivation for the assertion that one should live life fully. Existentialism suggests that all humans carry the awareness of their eventual death, and avoiding this thought only provokes anxiety. Instead, one should embrace death as it creates a sense of freedom.

At first glance, the philosophy might seem to focus on negative emotions. In reality, it aims to affirm the joy of life and all that can be achieved. However, this realization comes only if one can let go of the belief that others hold the answers to how one should live. By encouraging you to focus on your own thoughts and needs, existentialism awakens your self-awareness. Instead of concentrating on everything around you, the focus should be on yourself. Ultimately, this is where you will find the answer to what makes you happy.

Existential philosophy does not believe that happiness in life is pre-ordained. The world holds no value until you give it one through your actions and the opportunities you choose to pursue. "You are free, therefore [you must] choose," as Jean-Paul Sartre said. What you do shapes your world and ensures constant personal development. This grants you the freedom to influence and create your own understanding of what your life should entail. This freedom comes with the responsibility to define what you consider a good life. Your paths in life will continually change, as you are not a static being but constantly evolving.

Another recurring theme in existentialism is the focus on the individual's ability to take action. Philosophers in this field believe that you should dare to act and dare to make mistakes. Otherwise, you will see yourself as a static being, just a part of a larger society that, as a result, will define who you are. The philosophy emphasizes recognizing your own freedom to act. However, it also asserts that you should acknowledge the freedom of others. Despite its focus on your own thoughts, existentialism does not advocate for selfish or self-absorbed behavior.

Since you reflect on your own existence, it must mean that others do the same. This should be acknowledged when choosing your path in life. Therefore, one should avoid treating people as objects, but rather see them as they are. This is an impossible task in modern society if we do not first understand our own person—

and thereby the actions that constitute our person—according to existentialist philosophers.

The Paradox of Plenty

THE DIFFERENT PHILOSOPHERS

In this book, I will highlight several key figures who have significantly shaped the existentialist movement. Special attention will be given to Søren Kierkegaard, Friedrich Nietzsche, Jean-Paul Sartre, and Albert Camus, with each philosopher featured in their own section. These four were chosen for their substantial influence on existential philosophy and their insights on how we manage the opportunities and the actions of life which they require. This aspect is especially relevant to the themes of the book.

I will not focus heavily on their philosophical differences, such as Kierkegaard's support for religion or Sartre's atheism.[16] This is because such distinctions are not relevant to the content and purpose of the book.

Aside from the four philosophers on which I will be focusing, there are other thinkers who have shaped existential philosophy. This group includes Simone de Beauvoir, Arthur Schopenhauer, Karl Jaspers, Gabriel Marcel, Edmund Husserl, Martin Heidegger, Fyodor Dostoevsky, and Franz Kafka. Each of these philosophers brings a unique perspective to the key themes of existentialism. However, to keep the book focused on using existentialist ideas tackling the modern dilemma of choice, I will focus primarily on the mentioned four philosophers.

---

16   J. Gosetti-Ferencei (2021). *On Being and Becoming: An Existentialist Approach to Life An Existentialist Approach to Life*. Oxford University Press.

Existentialist philosophy is complex and cannot be boiled down to a few simple ideas or a single book. The thoughts of all these philosophers, along with others, often revolve around similar issues, particularly the concept of freedom and its meaning for individuals.

Existentialism is not a single, unified philosophy. To use it as a tool or a guide in modern life, we need to acknowledge its approach to grasping life's sometimes absurd aspects, our awareness of death—and the anxiety associated with our choices. It also requires recognizing how the philosophy tries to offer us hope and the will to pursue joy in life.

In the following sections, I will introduce four key philosophers of existentialism.

Søren Kierkegaard (1813–1855)

The Danish philosopher Søren Kierkegaard is often referred to as the father of existential philosophy. His ideas have had a significant influence on many philosophers who came after him, including Sartre and Camus, both of whom acknowledged the strong inspiration they drew from his works.

I believe that Kierkegaard's view of life can help put our daily habits and routines into perspective. As we navigate a world filled with countless options demanding our attention, we can turn to his writings that echo many thoughts which we all carry. This is particularly true when we find ourselves pondering the meaning of our lives. Few philosophers have delved as deeply into the significance of our self-perception as Kierkegaard.

Despite growing up in a wealthy family in Copenhagen, death was a constant presence in Kierkegaard's life. By the age of 22, he had lost five siblings, which may partly explain why the theme of death is prevalent in most of his texts. Other recurring themes include the human sense of anxiety when faced with life's manifold choices.

Like other philosophers highlighted here, Kierkegaard also rejected the notion that humans are born with a predetermined destiny. In his texts, he urges people to recognize that the frameworks we set for life can limit us. He critically examines our relationships with work, family life, and love. He does not suggest that these are wrong or should be avoided but rather that we should critically assess the value we attribute to our relationships with them. Especially when we engage in actions and choose a certain way of life without questioning why we do it or the value and joy it brings us. Often, we follow societal norms without giving them much thought. His ideas can offer valuable insights into our modern lives, where many of us automatically assume that the goal of life is to find love, settle in a beautiful home, and secure a successful career.[17]

---

17   Ferguson, R. (2013). *Life Lessons from Kierkegaard.*

Let's apply Kierkegaard's thoughts to a modern scenario. Remember the last time you bought a new phone? Did you find yourself spending hours reading all the reviews before making the purchase? This is quite normal. We often do this to minimize the doubt typically associated with buying something new. We strive to ensure that the product which we choose is the absolutely right one. This not only influences our behavior before the purchase, but also afterwards.

Once we make a decision, we usually face a sense of anxiety related to the need to make a choice. We buy the latest iPhone but cannot resist reading all the reviews after the purchase. Why? Because we fear we should have chosen the new Samsung phone instead. Similarly, we cannot help but check if we could have found our new phone for a lower price, even if we cannot return it anymore. It seems illogical, but we cannot help it. We must do everything to reassure ourselves that this particular decision—to buy the new iPhone—was the right one. This example illustrates the anxiety often associated with our decisions, a point Kierkegaard emphasizes. We cannot escape this anxiety; it is a normal part of being a free person with options and the ability to make decisions. In modern society, this anxiety accompanies us daily through the decisions we are compelled to make.

The above example highlights the anxiety we link to our choices because our choices are fraught with risk and uncertainty. As a result, we feel anxious, and Kierkegaard was the first to connect our uncertainty and anxiety with our choices. He articulated this as: "anxiety is the reality of freedom as a possibility for possibility."[18]

In his works, Kierkegaard explains that our anxiety is a condition of our existence, unfolding as we discover our own freedom and the multitude of possibilities it presents. He believes this anxiety is inherently linked to our freedom.

---

18   Translated from Danish. From the book Kierkegaard, S. (1844). *Begrebet Angest.*

Kierkegaard argues that when faced with freedom and the ensuing anxiety, we should not suppress these feelings. Instead, we are ultimately compelled to make a choice. If we try to avoid our freedom, the anxiety only grows because we have become aware of our freedom but choose not to utilize it. By repressing our freedom, we live a life filled with anxiety.

According to Kierkegaard, anxiety is inescapable. Every choice comes with risk and uncertainty because we cannot predict the outcome of our decisions. However, we must make choices to live our lives. Our feeling of anxiety is inevitable because it is part of our freedom. In his words, anxiety is the "dizziness of freedom." as he describes it.[19]

Kierkegaard wanted us to question what is important to us. By thinking about this, he believed we could live our best lives. He thought that the essence of being human lies in making choices. Shaping ourselves through these choices naturally involves feelings of anxiety. This anxiety, Kierkegaard would say, comes from being aware of our options. Only by facing our options and acting on them can we consider ourselves truly free. This is especially true for modern people, who face more options than ever but must make decisions to seize their freedom, as Kierkegaard would argue.

To be free, we should not look for answers from others, as this might mean giving up our freedom. Kierkegaard, like other existentialist philosophers, was worried about how a person can stay true to themselves in a modern society. Even in the 19th century, he was concerned about popular culture and its impact on our ability to be ourselves. Even though there was no internet, social media, or global trade in his time, he saw the first signs of mass culture. He wrote about the opening of Tivoli in 1843.

Over 10,000 people visited Tivoli in the capital of Denmark, Copenhagen, on its opening day, about a tenth of the city's popu-

---

19   Kierkegaard, S. (1844). *Begrebet Angest.*

lation at that time. During that summer, Tivoli had over 300,000 visitors, nearly a quarter of the total population. This showed the early rise of mass culture, something Kierkegaard found interesting and concerning.[20] It was an unprecedented gathering of people, impressive in many ways. However, this did not please Kierkegaard, who was highly critical of the idea that "the crowd is untruth."[21]

Kierkegaard did not believe that one should be isolated from society to live an authentic life. Instead, he thought it essential to engage with one's surroundings while being sincere in interactions with others. We should understand ourselves well enough not to let other people and the mass culture of modern society make us anonymous. If that happens, we lose ourselves and, consequently, the ability to live a good life, according to Kierkegaard.

Friedrich Nietzsche (1844–1900)

Friedrich Nietzsche also played a pivotal role in paving the way for existentialism. He believed that we, as humans, are capable of overcoming any challenge, as long as we are honest with ourselves. He expressed this idea with the phrase: "My humanity is a constant self-overcoming," which suggests that we are always evolving. Nietzsche argued that through this continuous development, if we can change our perception of our lives, we can become the person we truly are. These thoughts are a common thread in existentialism, which consistently focuses on the individual.[22]

Nietzsche was not an advocate of human herd mentality. He believed that we instinctively gravitate towards groups for a sense of security. However, he argued that we should resist this urge because it can trap us in a moral code that limits our ability to live our own lives. As part of a group, Nietzsche thought that we risk

---

20   Gosetti-Ferencei, J. (2021). *On Being and Becoming: An Existentialist Approach to Life An Existentialist Approach to Life.*

21   Egelund Møller, A. (1975). *Søren Kierkegaard om politik.*

22   "My humanity is a constant self-overcoming." from the book Nietzsche, F. W. (2017). *The Will to Power.*

having our actions dictated by others. Therefore, it is essential to find a balance between the comfort provided by our society and the control it can exert over our behavior. This is especially true for those who do not fit into the frameworks and norms set by the group and thus risk exclusion. Nietzsche saw this dynamic as inevitable in any group setting.

In his writings, Nietzsche focuses on how to find joy in life. He particularly believed that we should not always take the easy path in life, but rather one that also presents challenges. He explains that we need to be prepared for feelings of isolation, as standing against the crowd and facing our thoughts and challenges alone is necessary. If we cannot do this, we become dependent on others when life becomes difficult. And it will, at some point. Understanding and navigating these aspects of life are crucial, according to Nietzsche. If one cannot be alone and dare to go against the crowd, true freedom cannot be found. This doesn't mean we should isolate ourselves and not interact with others. However, Nietzsche argued that we shouldn't fear being alone with our thoughts and becoming independent of others. While living life as part of a larger social group is perfectly fine, we must acknowledge our own thoughts and understand that, in the end, we are alone. Our only reality is our own.[23]

Nietzsche's ideas remain relevant, especially regarding our need to fit in among others, which he believed contributes to our unhappiness. Like others in existentialism, he held that answers lie within ourselves and that it is dangerous to depend on others in the hope of finding happiness in life. He famously said, "Insanity in individuals is something rare—but in groups, parties, nations and epochs, it is the rule." This reflects his belief in the importance of individual thought and skepticism towards collective mindsets.

---

23   Nietzsche, F. W. (2018). *Schopenhauer as Educator.*

A common thread in both Nietzsche's and Kierkegaard's thoughts is their attempt to rescue the individual from becoming part of an ever-growing homogeneous mass, as represented by the culture we collectively create as humans. They both emphasized the importance of individuality and cautioned against losing oneself in the collective norms and values of society.

People's behavior changes depending on the situation, especially in larger groups where others' influence can lead to actions that might seem irrational in hindsight. For example, you might have been caught up in a trend and bought a pair of expensive shoes. At that moment, it felt like a good decision, but weeks later, you may stop wearing them and question your choice. Following shoe trends is a simple example. There are more serious cases where people collectively make poor choices. According to Nietzsche, we need to figure out what makes sense to us personally and then have the courage to follow that path. He emphasized the importance of thinking for ourselves, rather than being swayed by the crowd.

Jean-Paul Sartre (1905–1980)

Philosophy has often been considered irrelevant or reserved only for those who have the luxury to spend their time discussing life, not something applicable to real life. This was a common perception of philosophy until the existentialist movement gained prominence after World War II. Jean-Paul Sartre played a crucial role in popularizing this philosophy and putting it on the global map.

In the 1930s, philosophers like Jean-Paul Sartre and Simone de Beauvoir began developing a philosophy aimed at embracing life by questioning why and how we, as humans, choose to live. Before existentialism's rise, most people thought of philosophy as detached from reality, based on ideas not found in ordinary life, especially during the early years of World War II when Europe was under a dark cloud. It was precisely this context that gave existentialism a strong voice in society, both then and now, as philosophy suddenly became something people could incorporate into their lives.[24]

Sartre's existentialism revolves around the concept that all humans are inherently free. This freedom, however, is only realized when we detach ourselves from all presumptions about what defines us as humans. Our unique physical traits, cultural background, or personal histories do not necessarily define us. Instead, according to Sartre, we define ourselves through our actions. This notion forms the root of existentialism: it is our actions that shape our identity.

Sartre famously expressed this as "existence precedes essence." This means that we first exist, and then through our actions, we define our essence or identity. This was a groundbreaking idea, challenging the millennia-old belief that life's meaning was predetermined, often through religious doctrine. Sartre's statement that life starts without inherent meaning and only gains significance through our actions was both revolutionary and controversial.

He also introduced the concept of the 'absurd' to existentialism. This term does not suggest that life itself is absurd. Instead, it refers to the human quest for answers in a world that does not offer objective truths. We naturally seek meaning, yet we are left in a world devoid of predefined significance.

In our modern world, brimming with freedom and choices, we continue to search for answers. However, existentialists like Sartre suggest there is no ultimate answer. No definitive guide dictates which opportunities to seize for guaranteed happiness. Happiness, as per existentialism, is subjective, thus, its understanding must be individual.

Sartre also dwelt on the responsibility that comes with freedom, and the fear associated with the possibilities that freedom offers. He argued that the abundance of choices can make freedom seem daunting or even dangerous. To cope with this anxiety, he

---

24   Bakewell, S. (2017). *At the Existentialist Café.*

suggested, we often cling to predetermined assumptions about life, which, in turn, limit our true freedom. We tend to follow societal norms and roles without questioning them, which Sartre identified as living in 'bad faith'—a denial of life's inherent absurdity and our own freedom.

Thus, Sartre's existentialism is a call to embrace our freedom, recognize the absurdity of life, and define our essence through conscious actions and choices, resisting the temptation to fall into predetermined societal roles.[25] Sartre's philosophy emphasizes the inherent freedom given to every individual. This freedom is not something we have chosen; rather, it is an innate aspect of our existence. As such, we are 'condemned' to deal with it—to make choices and decisions in the absence of any predetermined guidelines. We are born into a world without explicit directions for our freedom, compelling us to forge our own moral compass.

This perspective leads Sartre to argue that answers to life's questions cannot be found through external authorities, be it religious institutions, government systems, parental guidance, or any other external influence. Since these authorities are composed of humans, they are no more equipped with universal truths or answers than any individual. In Sartre's view, each person must seek out their own truths and meanings.

The existential challenge, then, is to navigate life's ambiguities and complexities without relying on prescribed norms or values. Each person must take responsibility for their choices and the moral frameworks they live by, recognizing that their freedom is both a burden and an opportunity to define their existence.

Albert Camus (1913–1960)

Albert Camus, although distinct from Sartre in not explicitly identifying with existentialism, is nonetheless seen as a significant figure

---

25   "Man is condemned to be free" from the book: Sartre, J. (2007). *Existentialism is a Humanism.*

within the movement. His works explore similar themes central to existential philosophy, particularly the notion of life gaining meaning through personal attribution.

Growing up in Algeria, then a part of France, Camus believed that life was inherently absurd and devoid of meaning until we assign it significance. Despite his view of life's inherent meaninglessness, Camus's writings often emphasized the joys of living and the importance of savoring life's small moments. He advocated for the appreciation of friendships, love, music, and dance, positioning himself as a proponent of freedom and encouraging people to think beyond the constraints of life's established structures.

Camus's influence in popularizing existentialist thought extended beyond academic circles. His appeal reached wider audiences, as evidenced by his contact with Vogue magazine for a cover feature. He became a popular figure in the existentialist movement, much like Sartre, but in his unique way.

One of Camus's early works tells the story of a French coastal town in Algeria hit by a plague. The residents initially deny the plague's seriousness, downplaying its potential impact and continuing their lives focused on material gains without feeling truly alive. Camus critiques this mindset, suggesting that the townspeople are trapped in an illusion of immortality, driven by status and judgmental attitudes. Even as the plague intensifies and claims many lives, they remain in denial, convincing themselves of its insignificance. Camus uses this narrative to reflect on societal structures, where individuals live absurd lives, governed by trivialities. In his philosophy, the plague is a metaphor for the existential crisis everyone faces, captured in his statement,

> "Everyone has it inside himself, this plague, because
> no one in the world, no one, is immune"[26]

---

26   Camus, A. (2021). *The Plague.*

Camus believed that an invisible plague constantly pursues everyone, representing life's unpredictability. This plague, he argued, should not be ignored, as doing so leads to an absurd existence where actions are focused on ultimately meaningless pursuits like wealth, status, and recognition. For Camus, such pursuits are not conducive to a good and authentic life.

The theme of the absurd in life is a prominent aspect of Camus's work. Both he and Sartre agreed that humans are incapable of comprehending life's meaning, as, in their view, life inherently lacks a predefined purpose. However, they diverged on whether individuals could create meaning within this absurdity. Camus suggested that small joys in life could provide meaning, while Sartre argued that assuming an essence for life contradicts his belief that existence precedes essence.

Camus also held that certain essentials, like laws against violence, were necessary, and he believed self-love was a prerequisite for loving others. He articulated this notion in his statement: "That's the way man is, cher monsieur. He has two faces: he can't love without self-love."

This perspective highlights the importance which Camus placed on individual agency and self-understanding as key to navigating the inherent absurdity of life.[27]

Camus's perspective on life's absurdity emphasizes the importance of embracing life fully, despite its inherent meaninglessness. He advocated for a deep engagement with one's own existence, cultivating self-love as a foundation for living authentically and sharing love with others.

According to Camus, acknowledging life's absurdity is not a call to despair but an invitation to live more intensely and authentically. By investing in our personal growth and self-understanding, we can create a life of value and meaning, even in the face of absurdi-

---

27   Camus, A. (1991). *The Fall.*

ty. This approach encourages us to break free from societal norms and expectations that may confine us and to pursue a life that truly resonates with our individual desires and beliefs.

In essence, Camus argued for a courageous approach to life, one where we fully engage with our existence and the world around us, even if this world does not offer inherent meaning. By doing so, we can construct a fulfilling life, not in spite of life's absurdity, but through our response to it.

WHAT THE PHILOSOPHY OFFERS YOU

You have now read about four of philosophy's most pivotal figures. In their own ways, they each strive to prompt us to consider what the meaning of life is. They do not attempt to provide a definitive answer to what the meaning of life is, as according to them, there is no single, objective answer that fits everyone. This is something we must figure out for ourselves. Nevertheless, their ideas offer a range of perspectives on life that can assist us in focusing on ourselves, so we can evaluate which choices we wish to make and which choices bring value to our lives.

In the next section, you will find a summary of the most important perspectives shared by the four philosophers described above, which I will relate to throughout the rest of the book.

1. Humanity is free

All four philosophers refer in their own ways to the significance of our freedom and the importance of maintaining authenticity and the responsibility to dare to seize the opportunities freedom offers. In this way, they all illuminate the question of the meaning of life while also stating that the challenges and uncertainties that come with life are entirely normal. They describe how all people harbor the same thoughts because these thoughts are part of being human. Therefore, it is not about fleeing from life, but daring to explore it instead.

Humanity is free, which is their fundamental focus. Although you cannot control everything in your life, life unfolds based on the choices you make and the commitments you give yourself. You may not like it, but as existentialist philosophy says, you are responsible for creating the life you want. The same applies to the person you want to become. But having all the responsibility placed on oneself can seem daunting. It is daunting, according to existentialist authors. However, it is important to remember that the basis of our joy is subjective. Therefore, there is no right or wrong when figuring out what makes one happy.

2. Freedom creates anxiety

We all seem to live with the hope of being able to live a good and meaningful life. However, we are aware that we only have this one life, which is why we also do not want to waste it. But our awareness of this can often lead to anxiety about life, as we constantly doubt whether our current actions will benefit us later in life. This anxiety is about how we choose to live our lives. The way humans handle our freedom is what existentialism focuses on.

Existentialism takes it upon itself to outline what it means to live a life with freedom, joy, and authenticity. This is a task that in modern society seems like a complicated endeavor, as we are constantly faced with new opportunities and choices that need to be made. We know we need to make these choices, but doing so also creates anxiety about what our choices will mean for the future. As American psychiatrist Barry Schwartz describes, it is hard to choose among one's options, and choosing the right options seems to be even harder. Not least of all, it must be said to be a near-impossible task to choose the right options in a world full of endless possibilities.[28]

---

28   Schwartz, B. (2004). *The Paradox of Choice. Why More is Less. How the Culture of Abundance Robs Us of Satisfaction.*

3. Everyone and everything changes

Existentialism challenges the idea that life is stable and unchanging. It teaches that how we see ourselves and the world around us is not fixed but changes over time. The philosophy argues against seeing everything as unchangeable, saying that this viewpoint keeps us from truly understanding life. Instead, existentialism sees life as always moving and changing. Just as our bodies change over time, so do our minds.

Our minds are full of constantly changing thoughts and feelings, shaped by what we experience. Our whole existence is about change—from the moment we are born until we die. Change is the only thing we really know. Anything else is just a story we tell ourselves. Deep down, we understand that we cannot find the answers to life in other people or groups. We might naturally lean toward things like religion and social norms for comfort, but these can only give us a false sense of security. According to existentialism, everything is always changing, which means our identity is always evolving too.

4. Suffering is a part of life

Being human means being free. But freedom also means having the enormous responsibility to use it well. Thinking about this responsibility can sometimes make us feel bad. We might feel happy one moment and then remember that we have not achieved our dreams. Nevertheless, existentialism says we should not get stuck in this feeling. Instead, we should realize that feeling bad is a natural and important part of being free.

Different from other ways of thinking, like Stoicism, which deals with the fear of freedom by controlling our emotions, existentialists believe we should not fight or ignore feeling bad. Even if it is hard to think about life's randomness or the pain of thinking about death, they say that feeling bad is a necessary part of being human. Facing these tough thoughts can actually help us live better lives. It can make us more willing to act and try new things, knowing that life has an end.

5. Being true to oneself

Existentialism strives to create authentic individuals who take responsibility for the life they want to live. It suggests that we risk losing our own identity when we are among others. In larger gatherings, we become part of a homogeneous mass and forget to question our own actions.

For instance, have you ever taken the morning train to work? Packed among other passengers, all heading to their jobs, you might feel lost in the crowd. In that moment, you might forget your own thoughts and see yourself as part of a larger entity. You adopt an identity shared with everyone on the train, but it is not truly yours. Perhaps you have found yourself clapping along in a crowd because others did, not because you felt moved to. This mindset suggests that the crowd defines how we behave, posing a real risk for those who wish to live authentically with their own identity.

6. Others are also free

In our pursuit of authenticity and contemplation of our own freedom, we might forget that others are also free. We know we depend on others for essentials like food and water, but we often overlook how much we depend on others for our identity. Without others, we have no identity, as it is shaped by how they perceive us.

We often feel misunderstood, believing others see us only through their version of who we are. At its extreme, we might feel objectified, forgetting that these same people have their own thoughts, hopes, and dreams. For instance, when receiving a package, we might not consider the courier's aspirations, seeing them just as a postal worker. Thus, we constantly objectify others unintentionally. Living authentically means relating to others, recognizing their freedom and the possibilities in their lives.

Using existentialism

As you will see in the next part, existentialist philosophy can reduce some of the complications described in the section on the difficulty of choosing. It offers essential perspectives for the individual. Failing to reflect on our actions can lead to neglecting our freedom. We might feel trapped in actions not chosen by us, living unauthentically. Existentialism encourages us to actively engage with our choices, recognizing the freedom and responsibility they entail.

The result is reflected in our mental health, which in many aspects has shown a negative trend as the number of our choices has increased. The connection between our opportunities and mental well-being will be explained in the following part of the book, particularly focusing on why we struggle so much with making choices and how this can affect the way we see ourselves.

PART 4:
THE PROBLEM WITH CHOOSING

"Man is nothing else but what he makes of himself."
–Jean-Paul Sartre

THE VALUE OF OUR CHOICES

When was the last time you regretted something, you did? You may have felt this right after making a decision, or perhaps the regret surfaced later. Maybe a few days passed before you started to think about what else you could have done. Looking back, there might have been more alternatives to your choice, making you doubt your past actions as you consider the value of the decision you made.

Choosing among our options means both selecting and rejecting. We understand we cannot choose everything in life, but accepting this is another matter. Because for everything we select, we are left pondering over what we have given up. This process makes us focus on what we are missing, rather than what we have. As humans, we attribute value to the choices we make. And as our options increase, we become more aware of how to derive the most value from them.

But there is a difference between considering which decision to make and living with the fear of making the wrong one—just because another choice might have brought more value. When we do this, we are asking ourselves the wrong question.

**Instead of asking "what do I feel like doing?",
we have started asking ourselves, "what would be
the best thing for me to do?".**

Understanding the difference between these two questions is crucial. The first is centered on our personal desires, while the latter is based on others' perspectives. Before we make any decision, existentialism encourages us to always consider our own thoughts. To truly include ourselves in our decisions, we need to start by examining the value we assign to our choices—and importantly, why.

We can utilize a concept from economics called *opportunity cost* to understand how we evaluate the value of our actions. This concept explains how we consider the value of the opportunities we miss as a cost of our decision. Our choices, therefore, have a "price," and ideally, the choice should have a value higher than the opportunities it "costs." This term can help assess the value of one investment over another, but it can also be used to determine how we assign value to our choices and decisions.

For example, suppose you want to go on a holiday to Italy. The opportunity cost of choosing Italy is that you forego the option to visit France instead. Another opportunity cost is seen in the fact that the money spent on an Italian holiday cannot be used for something else. Or perhaps you are about to apply for a higher education course. In this case, your opportunity cost might include forgoing the chance to apply for other courses, as well as losing the opportunity to take a break, travel, or do something completely different.

Every decision we make, no matter how big or small, seems to have an opportunity cost associated with it. In other words, it comes with a cost. But if we overlook the impact this can have on us, we might be led astray because we are not aware of why we are making one decision over another. Opportunity costs seem to follow us everywhere in the choices we make. Maybe you choose to work late, which adds value to your job, but it also costs you time with your family. Another example could be getting invited to a football match but having a prior arrangement with your partner.

Regardless of your choice, there is a cost involved. You might gain a great experience from the football match but lose time spent with your partner.

When faced with a difficult decision involving multiple opportunity costs, we often start weighing and analyzing to find the best choice. You might have made a pros and cons list, a classic embodiment of opportunity costs, in hopes that the advantages of your decision will outweigh the disadvantages. However, it is not always that simple. Our choices are often more complex, raising the question: as our options increase, are we becoming too analytical, losing sight of what we really want?

Imagine you recognize the total cost of all the opportunities you say no to. You feel the lost value of not spending time with your family because you are working late. You also feel the lost value of choosing a football match over time with your partner. Now imagine it was not just a single alternative you missed out on when making your choice. Instead, you had hundreds of alternatives.

Not only did you miss time with your partner, but also a family birthday party, a relaxing day on the sofa, and several other possibilities. In theory, you could choose from an infinite number of options. Acknowledging the abundance of your alternatives is the same as recognizing the full potential of your freedom and opportunities.

Feeling the full weight of your options is not always pleasant. Yet, this is what we do every time we face a decision. We can fall into the trap of believing there is a perfect choice out there and that we can analyze our way to it—like with our lists of pros and cons. However, this is usually not possible.

Research in consumer behavior suggests that we are often more satisfied with our choices when we do not try to analyze the best decision, but instead go with the option that seems "good enough." The time lost in overanalyzing typically is not worth it.

In relation to the concept of opportunity cost, one could argue that the mental energy spent constantly evaluating the value of one's actions is, in itself, also an opportunity cost. Our time and energy used in decision-making is a lost cost, as it could have been spent on something else. Should we perhaps think less and act more if we want to create the greatest value for our actions?

The fear of missing out

We seem to have developed a culture centered around the fear of missing out, commonly known as FOMO. This reflects our natural psychological need not to miss out on anything. However, with the rise of social media and technological advancements that keep us constantly connected, there is an increased pressure on individuals. We are always aware of what others are doing, leading us to question what we might be missing out on. This FOMO culture is fueled by our growing opportunities to compare ourselves with others.

In her book "Alone Together" (2011), author Sherry Turkle discusses the consequences of being more connected through the internet and social media. She explains how we have become fully connected as part of a global network, yet often fail to consider the implications of this interconnectedness. We are always available via email, chat, and phone calls. It is never been easier to contact others or be contacted. But Turkle points out that, paradoxically, we feel more distant from people despite being more connected to them than ever before.

We increasingly spend time on social media, creating a dual personality. Turkle notes that we create our own "digital identity" that showcases our best moments. However, when we face difficulties in real life, we often turn to this digital identity, which always seems to be doing well. We lean on this identity, which appears more controllable than our real selves.

This dichotomy contributes to anxiety, as we escape from reality and convince ourselves we cannot influence it. Turkle argues that to avoid the pitfalls of our digital identity, we should focus more on being physically present with others. Her research indicates that people need to feel presence and be with others, but in the digital world, they are less likely to act on this need. Instead, they remain in their digital realm, as it seems easier than dealing with reality.

The digital identity may offer temporary relief but can lead to psychological instability due to reliance on a fabricated persona. To maintain mental well-being, Turkle suggests balancing our digital and real-life interactions, emphasizing the importance of physical presence and genuine connections over digital ones.[29] You might recognize the urge to check what others are doing on social media. Perhaps you even post pictures yourself, always portraying a positive image. This tendency to present our best selves is common in the modern world, prompting us to consider how we engage with this behavior.

The consequences of a FOMO (Fear of Missing Out) culture can make us forget the importance of living in the present moment. For instance, imagine a couple, after a long week of work, treating themselves to dinner at a nice restaurant. Yet, shortly after sitting down, they find themselves scrolling through Facebook and Instagram. It is not necessarily that they do not want to be there with each other, but rather they cannot resist checking if there is something even more exciting happening elsewhere, shared online. They might wonder if others are having more fun, which makes them curious about others' activities. By doing so, they inadvertently devalue their own choice—in this case, the experience of dining out. Imagine if the couple had entered the restaurant without their phones and simply enjoyed each other's company. Without

---

29   Turkle, S. (2011) *Alone Together: Why We Expect More from Technology and Less from Each Other.*

checking social media or distracting themselves, they would not know what others were doing and would not compare themselves. Instead, they would be fully present and appreciate the value of their chosen experience.

A study focusing on young people revealed that FOMO can lead to several negative side effects, including stress, poor sleep, fatigue, and decreased self-esteem. The study also indicated that FOMO particularly affects those who struggle to stay present, as they are preoccupied with what they might be missing out on. This trend is closely linked to the increasing use of social media.[30]

Consider how the world was before the internet and social media. Imagine a time when you did not have to worry about your social media presence, when you were not constantly reminded of events you were missing, or bombarded with offers for dream vacations that made you long for escape.

Today's world seems quite different. We have developed a culture centered around the fear of missing out. The reality of a FOMO culture is inescapable.

The question, therefore, is not how to avoid this culture, but how to best navigate within it.

As highlighted, it is important to consider how we view our options before making a decision. But it is also relevant to examine how we react after making a choice. The previous section explained how we weigh our alternatives and opportunity costs to assign value to the options presented to us. We increasingly fear missing out, and as the number of choices grows, making the right decision becomes more challenging. Yet, we persist in trying. Instead of pausing and reflecting on our choices, we continue to seek new

---

30   Milyavskaya, M., Saffran, M., Hope, N. & Koestner, R. (2018). *Fear of missing out: prevalence, dynamics, and consequences of experiencing FOMO.*

opportunities. This trend is not necessarily the most optimal, as further explained below.

American professor Baba Shiv (2000) conducted research on how we respond after making a decision. He explains that our pursuit of the best in life creates a need to make more decisions. This is because we see value in our choices and thus, we want to make more of them, to maximize our potential gains. Our need to accomplish everything, according to Shiv, stems from the trap of constantly seeking our next decision to realize our next opportunity.

We understand that our options contain value we want to capture. This aligns with our FOMO culture, where we do not want to miss out. Hence, we fill our calendar with coffee appointments and social events, not wanting to miss the potential value they could offer. However, we often forget to stop and consider what we truly desire. In this process, we may find ourselves in a recurring cycle of chasing the next opportunity and decision, neglecting to appreciate what we already have. We seek only the value of the next choice, which can result in a never-ending sense of insufficiency.

Many of us are familiar with this feeling after achieving a goal we worked towards. Whether completing a major work project, finishing education, or running your first big race, what feeling typically lingers after reaching your goal? You might have just completed your education, but within days, you start pondering your next step. There is almost a fear of the unknown, with questions about your next choice emerging. You ask yourself, "What do I do now?", "Was my study choice right?", or "What if I can't find a job?". Our thoughts begin to shift towards what our next decision should be. If we fail to do this, we view ourselves as always lacking something.

In a study by Brant & Veroff (2007), it was discovered that individuals who reflected on things they were grateful for also experienced greater joy in life. The study highlighted that activities like focusing on the present, sharing thoughts with others, and congratulating oneself for good deeds contribute to appreciating what one already has.

Could it be that our inability to pause and consider what we already have contributes to feeling less content, even though we have more welfare and greater freedom? Additional studies indicate that as our options increase, we attempt to manage more decisions simultaneously. However, humans are not good at focusing on multiple things at once. Trying to handle more than we can leads to losing focus on our current tasks and the value they hold.

This scattering of attention can detract from our well-being, as we overlook the significance and enjoyment of what we already possess.[31] My belief is that there is significant benefit in focusing on just a few things at a time rather than spreading our attention across many options. If we don't, we risk not being fully engaged in the activities we do or the people we are with. Our entire life turns into a never-ending checklist, where even our social interactions become tasks to complete.

---

31   Shiv, B. & Huber, J. (2000). *The Impact of Anticipating Satisfaction on Consumer Choice.*

IRRATIONAL DECISIONS

As previously mentioned, modern research indicates that having fewer options and a concentrated focus can increase happiness. So why do we often do the opposite? According to Dan Ariely, an American professor of psychology and behavioral economics (2008), this is partly because we act more irrationally than we think, which affects our decision-making. His studies reveal how many of our actions, though seemingly irrational, are still carried out.

Ariely examines the idea that our decision-making is often flawed due to inherent biases and irrational behaviors. These flaws can lead us to make choices that do not serve our best interests or enhance our happiness and well-being. He suggests that recognizing and adjusting for these biases can lead to better decision-making. Ariely's work implies that by simplifying our choices and focusing on what is truly important, we can improve our life satisfaction and be more present in our daily experiences.[32]

Did you know we are more likely to wait in line at a restaurant with a long queue instead of choosing one without a line? We tend to assume something is good based on others' actions, reasoning that if people are willing to wait, the place must be worthwhile. But this is not always true. A line does not necessarily mean better food; it just seems more popular, leading us to think it is superior.

---

32 Ariely, D. (2008). *Predictably Irrational, Revised and Expanded Edition: The Hidden Forces That Shape Our Decisions.*

Consider walking into an empty restaurant. Without tasting the food, you might think less of it, simply because it lacks other diners. This reasoning, though common, is irrational, driven by our tendency to value our choices based on others' actions.

Ariely's research points out our irrational responses, often filling gaps in our understanding. For instance, in a study involving a fake painkiller, participants reported more pain relief when they thought the pill was expensive ($2.50) compared to when they believed it was cheap ($0.10). The pill was the same in both scenarios and not a real painkiller, yet the perceived price significantly altered its placebo effect.

This lack of rationality in decision-making is important to recognize, as it affects our choices. As the previous section of this book explains, we tend to make more decisions as our options increase. However, if we do not understand the real reasons behind these choices, we may end up making decisions influenced by what others want. For example, we might fill our calendar with unwanted appointments or wait in line at a popular new restaurant without really considering why.

Recognizing that we may not be as rational as we think, or as rational as we would like to be in valuing our actions, can be enlightening. If you have ever found yourself at a social event just because you felt you should, despite not wanting to, this is a classic example of irrational behavior. We often act against our desires, which, when examined, is not rational at all.

If we are convinced that external things bring value and meaning to our lives, we had better gain insight from existentialism, which suggests that we are the only ones who can assign value to our actions. The importance of your coffee date with a friend or a crucial work meeting is solely significant because you tell yourself it is. Instead of striving to accomplish as much as possible, existentialist thinking advises focusing on what you truly want to achieve. By doing so, you avoid assigning external things a value for your well-being and concentrate on your own values.

Drawing a parallel to consumer behavior research, we enjoy being presented with options. However, we can only appreciate these choices if we are not overwhelmed by too many at once. Overloading our schedule with appointments in the pursuit of numerous options can have adverse effects. We may believe we are being rational by equating more activities and appointments with a greater chance of not missing out and thus gaining more value. But in our pursuit, we forget how we manage our thoughts after making a decision. We need to become better at understanding how we influence our perception of our choices. If we don't, we will continuously feel something is missing.

Limiting ourselves

We usually tend to make decisions that are not necessarily in our best interest, and we do not always use rational thinking while making choices. One of the reasons is that we influence ourselves and how we view our choices, often to the point of confusing ourselves by trying to twist reality to fit our current values and attitudes.

This leads to cognitive biases impacting how we perceive our options. A cognitive bias is essentially a mental shortcut our brain uses to process the immense amount of information it receives daily, both from ourselves and our surroundings. These shortcuts help the brain process information more efficiently, but they also influence how we see our options and the choices we make.

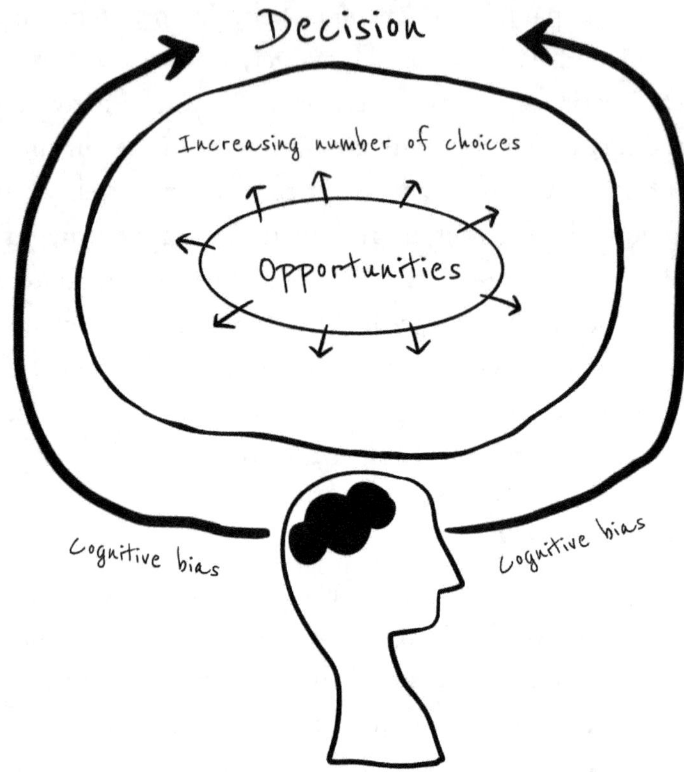

The objective of this section is to explain how cognitive biases can influence you to make irrational decisions and even lead you to believe that you have no options to choose from. By becoming aware of the mental shortcuts your brain takes when considering your options, you can better understand how they affect your decisions and, consequently, your reactions.

**Instead of being trapped in a perception of what
we think we should do, we should focus on what
we want to do.**

This requires awareness of how we influence ourselves. Without this self-awareness, we cannot focus on ourselves, which is also essential to existentialist thinking. However, this can be challenging when presented with numerous options, as our brain automatically falls into the trap of trying to influence our choices. It does this simply because it seeks the easiest and most apparently correct answer. But as we have learned, our first instinct is not always the best. To elaborate on this, there are five particular cognitive biases that significantly affect our decision-making. Becoming aware of these can help us understand why we sometimes react irrationally.

The five cognitive biases and self-imposed limitations are:

1) We struggle to let go
2) We get accustomed to what we have
3) We overvalue what is already ours
4) We resist change
5) We forget the potential gains

1. We struggle to let go

We often find it difficult to let go of decisions we have made, especially when we have already invested time, money, or emotions into them. This is explained by the concept of "sunk cost fallacy," which describes our tendency to cling to past choices due to our investment in them, even when it is no longer rational.

Take the example of staying in a movie theater to watch a film you are not enjoying, simply because you have already paid for the ticket and committed your time. The money and time spent are sunk costs—you cannot recover them, yet they still influence your decision to stay.

This phenomenon also shows up in dining experiences. You might feel compelled to finish your meal or eat as much as possible at a buffet just because you have paid for it. Even if you are full, the sunk cost of the payment pushes you to continue eating. It is a clear example of how sunk costs can sway our decisions, convincing us to act against our better judgment or desires.

Sunk cost fallacy can extend to our personal relationships as well. For instance, someone might struggle to leave an unhealthy relationship because they are focusing on the time and effort already invested. They may rationalize staying with their partner, citing years of history together, rather than recognizing this past time as a sunk cost that should not dictate their future choices.

Not being aware of how sunk costs trap us can lead to staying in situations that are not beneficial, out of fear of losing what we have already "invested." You have spent money on a movie ticket or a meal, but that expenditure should not influence your present decisions. Yet, often, it is hard not to let it. This fallacy shows that the more we invest in a decision, the harder it becomes to think clearly and let go, limiting our ability to freely choose among our options.

By focusing on how much we have invested in a decision, rather than how it truly serves us, we can lose sight of what is actually best for us. In the case of someone staying in an unhealthy relationship, they might feel trapped by the investment of time and emotions, even though they have the freedom to choose otherwise. Recognizing and overcoming the influence of sunk costs is crucial for making decisions that truly align with our desires and well-being.

2. We get accustomed to what we have

Do you remember the feeling you experienced the last time you put on a new pair of shoes? Or maybe the first time you drove a new car? Everything felt new, exciting, and incredibly valuable. You took care of your new shoes, and you made sure that your new car was always clean. But suddenly, it changed. You stopped taking care of your shoes and let them slowly get dirtier. The car became more cluttered, and it was no longer important that it was always clean. This describes how we can get used to what we have, a process known as adaptation. What is interesting is how this leads us to take things for granted. And through that, how it can lead us to make the wrong decisions.[33] As the existential philosopher Albert Camus said, "After a while, you could get used to anything."[34]

Often, the things we seek are never quite as satisfying as we hoped they would be. Perhaps you may have bought your new shoes for the thrill of shopping, rather than for the function they serve. You know, keeping your feet warm and dry.

But eventually, you realized they were just another pair of shoes. The same goes for your new car. Maybe you imagined how it would improve your life, but you quickly got used to your new comfortable (and significantly more expensive) seat and its brand-new air conditioning. Both the shoes and the car lost their effect on you because you got used to them.

We quickly adapt to what we have, which can lead us to fall into the trap of constantly seeking more. This can also make us feel the need to keep searching, even when we are content. Examples of this can be seen at work or in relationships, where we may feel the need for something new because, over time, we value them less. We have gotten used to how good we have it, which can lead us to feel that we should look for more, even though we are well off.

Adaptation can therefore lead to the trap of always believing that the grass is greener on the other side, as the saying goes. And maybe there is some truth to it? You might have experienced it yourself, feeling compelled to take a new job with higher pay because you suddenly feel the need for more.

You want new shoes again, or a new car, because you have gotten used to what you already have. Your needs evolve, which can be healthy, but it can also distract you from what truly makes you happy. Otherwise, we can constantly feel like we are missing something, as Baba Shiv described in the previous chapter, where we are always chasing more and more. However, there is strength

---

33   Frederick, S. & Loewenstein, G. (1999). *Hedonic adaptation.*

34   "After a while you could get used to anything.". Camus, A. (1989). *The Stranger.*

in being able to pause and reflect on what we already have, to avoid a perpetual cycle of always needing to acquire new things.[35]

3. We overvalue what is already ours

Imagine you have saved up for a concert ticket to see your favorite band. Suddenly, you find out you cannot attend and need to sell the ticket. How much would you sell it for? In similar cases, researchers have found that we often try to sell it for more than we paid. Suppose you paid $150 for the ticket; you might want to sell it for $200. You see the ticket as yours and do not want to part with it for the same price you paid for it.[36] The reason you feel it is okay to sell the ticket at a higher price is because you place a higher value on things that are your own. This behavior is explained by the concept known as the "endowment effect," which describes our tendency to value our own possessions more highly than others'.[37]

In an experiment by Jack Knetsch and Jack Sinden (1984), a group of participants were each given either $2 or a lottery ticket of the same value. After a while, one group was given the option to exchange their lottery ticket for money, and conversely, the other group could exchange their money for a lottery ticket. However, almost none of them chose to make the exchange, even though both items had the same value. In another experiment, participants were given a coffee mug and later offered the chance to exchange it for another item of equal value, like a pen. The findings showed that the participants wanted to be paid double the value of the coffee mug for the exchange. This experiment demonstrated how our sense of ownership leads us to overestimate the value of our

---

35   Frederick, S. & Loewenstein, G. (1999). *Hedonic adaptation.*

36   Weaver, R. & Frederick, S. (2012). *A reference price theory of the endowment effect.*

37   Kahneman, D., Knetsch, J. L. & Thaler, R. H. (1991) *Anomalies: The Endowment Effect, Loss Aversion, and Status Quo Bias.*

possessions. It also revealed that the participants saw the pen as less valuable because they did not own it.[38] [39]

In relation to the number of options we have, our sense of ownership can lead us to make irrational decisions. This may cause us to cling to things we already possess because we believe they are more valuable. For instance, in the case of the concert ticket, this belief may prevent you from selling it, as you might think it is worth more than its actual value. This mindset can also manifest in our thoughts about others, where we might believe our opinions and values hold more worth than those of others. In other words, we often think we are always right.

If we overestimate the value of what we already have, it can lead us to overlook what we do not have or what we are unfamiliar with. This understanding is also driven by the next cognitive bias, which suggests that we prefer things to remain the same.

4. We resist change

Change can be intimidating, leading many to desire that things remain the same. Psychology actually reveals that this is a cognitive bias where we try to maintain the *status quo*. Besides preventing us from seeking new opportunities, this bias also influences the choices we make.

Our *status quo* bias is the reason you do not switch your mobile plan even though it could save you money. It might only take a few minutes to switch, but it seems easier not to bother. Similarly, it is why you order food from the same take-out place, even though there are many other options available. Perhaps you even choose the same dish every time you order? All of these are signs of *status*

---

38   Knetsch, J. L. & Sinden, J. A. (1984). *Willingness to Pay and Compensation Demanded: Experimental Evidence of an Unexpected Disparity in Measures of Value.*

39   Kahneman, D., Knetsch, J. & Thaler, R. (2011). *Experimental Tests of the Endowment Effect and the Coase Theorem.*

quo bias, indicating our reluctance to risk losing something by trying something new.[40]

Have you ever been presented with a new opportunity but chose to say no because it seemed too troublesome? Perhaps you were offered a new job, an opportunity to travel, or were asked to try a new sport. Even though you wanted to try these things, you still told yourself it was not worth it. Most likely, it was your *status quo* bias telling you not to risk what you already have for something unknown.[41] When we follow this mindset, we try to limit what we might lose, but this also restricts the benefits we could gain from trying something new. It can also narrow our perspectives on topics like politics, where we risk choosing to vote for the same party we always have, because we do not want to be open to other viewpoints. The same applies to our eating habits and general health, where we prefer to stick to what we know.

In a study, it was even shown that people preferred to continue with their current medication, even when offered a new one that was better. This demonstrates that our desire not to change our current choices can prevent us from making better ones, simply because we are unfamiliar with them. Could it be that we prevent ourselves from realizing the best opportunities for us because we focus too much on what we might lose? Could this explain why our increasing number of choices might have a negative impact on our mental health?

5. We forget the potential gains

Would you rather avoid losing $1,000 than win $1,000? At first glance, it may seem like a trick question, as the amount is the same, so it should not matter. However, most people answer that they would rather avoid losing money than winning it. This is due to

---

40   Kahneman, D., Knetsch, J. L. & Thaler, R. H. (1991) *Anomalies: The Endowment Effect, Loss Aversion, and Status Quo Bias.*

41   Samuelson, W. & Zeckhauser, R. (1988). *Status quo bias in decision making.*

the cognitive bias known as *loss aversion*, which describes how the feeling of losing something can feel twice as bad as the feeling of winning something.[42]

Loss aversion explains how we can end up focusing on not wanting to lose rather than winning. In our daily lives, this can lead us to focus on holding onto what we have by making a series of choices that do not necessarily benefit our well-being. It is also this cognitive bias that partly drives a FOMO (Fear of Missing Out) culture, where we focus on everything we could miss out on. As a result, we try to do everything, which can also be seen as one of the reasons we want to make more decisions as the number of our options increases. We simply do not want to miss out on anything. In the context of our options, this can make us cling to the belief that we do not want to change our circumstances, even though they are bad for us. We may therefore focus more on what we could lose, rather than what we could gain.

As can be seen, we do not always act as rationally in our decisions as we might think. In fact, many of the choices we make can seem illogical because we are influenced by other people—and not least by ourselves. When we act irrationally, it is due to our desire to create the most value for the choices we make. But this can also limit us if we are not aware of it. As explained in the five cognitive biases, not knowing how we are influenced and what it means can have significant consequences for our lives.

However, it can seem challenging to focus on how both others and ourselves can influence our thoughts. You might recognize several cognitive biases in the way you make your own decisions. But it is one thing to become aware of what influences and limits you and it is another to do something about it. Fortunately, existential philosophy can help you focus on what you can do, rather than what you should not do. And thereby shift the focus to your-

---

42   Kahneman, D., Knetsch, J. L. & Thaler, R. H. (1991) *Anomalies: The Endowment Effect, Loss Aversion, and Status Quo Bias.*

self rather than others. However, it first requires that you reflect on how you limit yourself and your understanding of your options. Otherwise, you might focus too much on what you should do, rather than what you want to do.

In their own way, the cognitive biases describe how we can end up focusing on what we might lose instead of what we could gain. When we combine this understanding of our choices with a desire to acquire as much value as possible through our actions, we create a dangerous cocktail.

As you will read in the next section, this is evident in that we come to compare most of our choices. Instead of focusing on ourselves and our own desires, we may end up focusing on everyone else because we try to get as much value as possible from our choices. But this also leads to several negative consequences for how we see ourselves.

TO COMPARE YOUR CHOICES

The concept of how we compare ourselves to others was first introduced by the American psychologist Leon Festinger in 1954. He called it 'social comparison'. He believed that as humans, we need to judge ourselves and others because we try to analyze who we are. We compare ourselves to others to form a basis for how we can evaluate and understand ourselves in relation to others.[43]

Typically, we tend to compare ourselves with a group of people whose abilities we believe are similar to our own.

Here, the social comparison theory explains that we tend to compare ourselves either upward or downward.

If we compare ourselves with people whom we think are better than us, we are engaging in upward comparison. When we do this, we try to improve our own status and abilities to be like those we compare ourselves with. This can be motivating and have a positive effect, as it pushes us to strive for more. However, it can also lead to envy for what others have that we lack. When this happens, we feel inadequate because it creates a sense of missing something in our lives.

---

43   Festinger, L. (1954). *A theory of social comparison processes.*

Conversely, we can also compare ourselves downward when we look at people who are seemingly doing less well than ourselves.[44] It can be positive when it leads to a sense of gratitude for what we have. However, it can also be negative, if it makes us feel superior to others. For instance, you might walk past a homeless person and feel thankful for what you have in your life. In this scenario, your comparison could trigger a positive feeling, inspiring you to give back so others can have what you do. But you could also compare yourself with the homeless person and feel superior because you believe you have a better handle on your life. In such a case, your comparison leads to a negative impact.

Festinger believed that all people are dependent on comparing themselves with others. We need to do this to understand what we are good and bad at. However, there can also be several negative consequences when we compare ourselves with others. Constant upward comparisons can make our own lives seem deficient. By comparing yourself with others, you might forget to ask whether you even want the same things as the person you are comparing yourself to. Additionally, it can make you overlook what you already have, focusing instead on what you lack. When you engage in downward comparisons, you might get caught up in focusing on how you are better than others. This can lead you to believe that you always need to have the answer or even lie to others by telling yourself that you must be good at everything because you want to appear better than others.[45] But letting this be the driving force behind who you associate with and what you do will never create the framework for a good life. It will only contribute to limiting your own life because you cannot stop comparing yourself to others, existential philosophy would say.

---

44   Wang, J. L., Wang, H. Z.,Gaskin, J. & Hawk, S. (2017). *The Mediating Roles of Upward Social Comparison and Self-esteem and the Moderating Role of Social Comparison Orientation in the Association between Social Networking Site Usage and Subjective Well-Being.*

45   Pomery, E.A., Gibbons, F. X., Stock, M.L. (2012). *Social Comparison.*

A 2018 study shows that in most cases, we tend to compare ourselves upward. According to the study, we more often fill our lives with people we look up to. You might find yourself making upward comparisons with people who have more money, better health, better relationships, and so on.

The problem with this tendency, as the study indicates, is that it makes us feel inadequate.[46] Striving for more can be advantageous when we need to perform, but it is not beneficial for our mental well-being. If we are always looking upward, we lose perspective on our past achievements, while setting impossible standards for ourselves.

The consequences of upward comparison are particularly evident through our use of social media. In a study examining how we are influenced by Facebook, 80 test participants were divided into two groups. One group browsed their Facebook newsfeed for 15 minutes, while the other group looked at National Geographic's Facebook page for the same duration. Both test groups used Facebook as a platform, but only those who scrolled through their newsfeed were exposed to social comparison.

Individuals who could compare themselves to others showed signs of lower self-esteem and a higher degree of depressive thoughts than those who did not make such comparisons.[47]

Shifting focus away from ourselves

A common aspect of our way of comparing ourselves is that it diverts focus away from us. We let other individuals become the focus, allowing them to help define who we are. According to ex-

---

46   Gerber, J. P., Wheeler, L. & Suls, J. (2018). *A social comparison theory meta-analysis 60+ years on.*

47   Yitshak, A. (2019). *The grass is always greener on my Friends' profiles: The effect of Facebook social comparison on state self-esteem and depression.*

istentialist philosophy, we should concentrate on ourselves to find meaning. By comparing ourselves to others, we choose to do the opposite. Yet, this seems to be part of human nature, which we need to acknowledge and address.

As previously mentioned, we compare ourselves to establish a basis for how we perceive ourselves. However, when we compare our lives to what others have, we may start viewing our own lives as empty. This is particularly true when using social media, which several studies have linked to a negative self-perception leading to anxiety and depression.[48][49]

Just as with our actions, where we try to choose those with the greatest value, we also seem to attempt to compare ourselves based on the same principle: we want to appear in the best possible light, both to ourselves and to others. But what is the connection between our choices and the way we present ourselves?

A theory, called *self-discrepancy.* explains how people maintain several different perceptions of themselves. In other words, we hold onto an understanding of who we really are, who we would like to be, and importantly, who we think we should be. This theory was developed by Tory Higgins (1987) and helps explain how we build a series of discrepancies within ourselves.[50] Perhaps you tell yourself that you should earn more than you currently do. In such a case, there is a discrepancy between your understanding of your current situation and how you would like it to be. When we compare ourselves to others, similar discrepancies come to the surface. For instance, you might compare yourself to a colleague whom you believe earns more than you. In this case, you are comparing upwards, which can drive you to strive for the same as your colleague,

---

48   Tandoc, E. C.,Ferrucci, P. & Duffy, M. (2015). *Facebook use, envy, and depression among college students: Is facebooking depressing?*

49   Shaw, A. M., Timpano, K. R., Tran, T. B. & Joormann, J. (2015). *Correlates of Facebook usage patterns: the relationship between passive Facebook use, social anxiety symptoms, and brooding.*

50   Higgins, E. (1987). *Self-Discrepancy: A Theory Relating Self and Affect*

or it might lead to envy. Either way, you tell yourself something is lacking in your life.

We look towards others to understand ourselves

It appears that we compare ourselves with others to understand ourselves, but in the process, we often present ourselves in ways that do not reflect our true selves. When our choices are influenced by this need to look to others, how can we be satisfied with our decisions if we are constantly comparing them to others'?

In a study by Matthew Baldwin and Thomas Mussweiler (2018), the two researchers describe how we are creating a culture of comparison. They also believe that humans cannot avoid comparing themselves to others, but that in modern society, it has led to a behavior where we are more inclined to compare everything we do with others. They explain that because it is easier for us to see what others do, it has also become easier to compare our actions. As humans, we use our social skills to coordinate how we should behave in social contexts. We look to others to understand how we should act, as well as how we should think and feel.[51]

To understand the significance of how we let others influence our choices, let's conduct a thought experiment. Think back to the last time you spent the entire weekend binge-watching Netflix. At the moment, it felt really good, until you had to tell your friends how you spent your weekend or until you scrolled through your social media and found out that all your friends spent their weekend at fun and exciting events. Suddenly, you feel like your weekend was wasted because you should have spent it on something more sensible.

Now, imagine instead that you live in a world where there are no others to consider or compare yourself with. How would you then think about your weekend on the couch? I know it is an unrealistic scenario, but you would most likely be completely indif-

---

51   Baldwin, M. & Mussweiler, T. (2018). *The culture of social comparison.*

ferent to thoughts about what you should do. Instead, you would prioritize what you want to do, what you needed to do. Could it be that we are losing the ability to define ourselves, as we increasingly try to compare ourselves with others?

A desire to fit in

Why do we look to others when comparing our choices? Author James Clear (2018) believes the answer lies in humanity's biological past, based on the idea that we are all born as herd animals. Therefore, it is instinctual for us to want to fit in with others in the herd. Thus, we strive to gain respect and recognition from our social circles, as it has been essential for our survival in the past. We do not have to go many thousands of years back in human history, since it was necessary to live together in tribes to survive. And to increase one's chances of survival, one had to be a member of the tribe, which required fitting in. Being ostracized from the tribe was the same as a death sentence.[52]

Today, we are not as dependent on each other as we used to be. So, our natural drive for social acceptance shows up in ways that can limit how independent we are. Psychologist Steven Pinker (2013) explains that people often adopt values that win them the most social approval. This happens even more than sticking to values we truly believe in.[53] In modern society, this understanding still resides within us. We cannot bear the thought of not receiving recognition from others, as it is associated with being excluded from our tribe and thereby risking our own safety. As a result, we would rather downplay our own values to fit in and gain acceptance in a social circle.

In a classic experiment by Solomon Asch (1951), it was demonstrated that people would rather lie and fit in with the social group

---

52   Clear, J. (2018). *Atomic Habits: An Easy & Proven Way to Build Good Habits & Break Bad Ones.*

53   Pinker, S. (2013). *Language, Cognition, and Human Nature: Selected Articles.*

than tell the truth and risk standing out. Asch illustrated this in an experiment where he showed test subjects three lines of different lengths. He surrounded the test subjects with a group of people who had been instructed to say that all three lines were of equal length. When the test subjects were asked to state their answers, it turned out that 70% of them said the lines were of equal length. Even though the test subjects could see that the three lines were of different lengths, they preferred to lie in order to fit in. They chose to conform to the group's answer, even though they knew it was wrong. The study thus showed that humans will lie in order not to risk standing out.[54]

In a 2004 study, researchers investigated how the sense of community and the value of a brand can influence the value we derive from a product. For their experiment, they chose to examine the difference in taste experience between Coca-Cola and Pepsi. When it comes to marketing, the choice between these companies is obvious, as they have had one of the longest-running marketing battles against each other (and still do to this day). This battle has even been named the "Cola Wars," where both parties aim to win consumers' association with cola.[55] The study aimed to determine which of the two companies, Coca-Cola or Pepsi, people think of when they hear the word "cola". Researchers set up a simple experiment to investigate the effect of the two brands on taste experience, essentially determining which one tasted better. Initially, participants conducted a blind taste test where they stated a preference for the taste of Pepsi. However, when allowed to see which of the two they were drinking, they suddenly preferred the taste of Coca-Cola, which seems illogical given that the same people had just expressed a liking for Pepsi. The study showed that the social

---

54   Asch, S. E. (1951). *Effects of group pressure upon the modification and distortion of judgments.* In H. Guetzkow (Ed.), Groups, leadership and men; research in human relations (s. 177–190).

55   History.com (2022). *https://www.history.com/news/cola-wars-pepsi-new-coke-failure*

connotation associated with drinking Coca-Cola rather than Pepsi held greater value, leading people to prefer it even though they did not find it as tasty as Pepsi.[56]

Perhaps we see a similar influence in our everyday life? Socially accepted food items, clothing brands, and so forth, influence all of us to choose options that our social circle deems most valuable. Thus, the choices we make affect whether we fit in or not. As the experiment shows, the joy and value we attribute to our choices are subjective. When Coca-Cola's brand was removed from the equation of what tasted best, Pepsi won. However, this changed when the perception of others regarding one's actions re-entered the equation.

Humans are raised to adapt. We would rather compromise our values and even lie to others to fit in. In modern society, where we often compare ourselves more with others, this can lead to numerous problems. Suppose you are about to make a decision. You have already decided what you want to do, but at the last minute, you find out that everyone else has chosen to do the opposite. What do you do?

As one of the above studies shows, most of us would change our minds and do what others are doing. We see this manifested in many aspects of our daily life, where we lean towards what other people in our social circle do. This is what existentialism would describe as an inauthentic life, where one denies their freedom to think for themselves and then perform the action they truly desire. We will return to this in the final part of the book.

The pursuit of status

How do you introduce yourself to a new person? Do you start by mentioning where you work and your job title? If so, you are not alone. When getting to know someone new, many of us try to

---

56   McClure, S. M., Li, J., Tomlin, D., Cypert, K., Montague, L. & Montague, P. (2004). *Neural Correlates of Behavioral Preference for Culturally Familiar Drinks.*

compare ourselves with them. We use things like our profession and career path to indicate our status to others. We can become dependent on this pursuit of status, leading us to make decisions that contradict our own desires. If we are not aware of this pursuit, we might prioritize how we appear to others and forget our authentic needs and desires.

Robert H. Frank, in his book "Choosing the Right Pond: Human Behavior and the Quest for Status" (1985), emphasizes how much our social life is governed by our desire to achieve status. He explains that we all compare ourselves with a reference group of people who are significant in our lives. We do not compare ourselves with everyone on earth, as that would make us seem insignificant in the grand scheme. Instead, we select a reference group where we strive to be successful. This could be your social circle, where you might want to appear successful to your friends. But we all have various reference groups, so you will also try to present your best self to your family, colleagues, or members of your local football club. Wherever you create your reference group, as a human, you aim to appear successful to them. As Frank describes, we choose to find a group and stay there to pursue our mission among the same people. Ask yourself, how do you try to appear to your colleagues, family, and friends? How do you want them to see you? And why is it important?

In a 1998 study, Sara Solnick and David Hemenway explored the significance of having status through an experiment that posed a simple question to participants: Would they prefer a job that paid $50,000 a month while their colleagues earned $25,000? Or would they rather earn $100,000 a month while their colleagues earned $200,000? The job entailed exactly the same tasks. The only difference was how much they would earn compared to their colleagues. The experiment showed that over 50% of participants chose to earn $50,000 rather than $100,000. It seems illogical that they would prefer to earn less, but their need to appear better than their reference group weighed more than the money. They preferred to earn less as long as it was more than what their colleagues earned. Why? Because it made them appear more successful than their reference group. They valued status more than money.

As the study shows, we do not always think rationally about our actions when comparing ourselves to others. Often, we are influenced by our need to appear as good as possible. In a modern reality filled with choices, it is crucial to be aware of how our need to compare can lead us to prioritize some decisions over others. In the experiment mentioned, the rational choice would have been to take the job that paid the most. Yet, over half chose the opposite.

We tend to compare ourselves with others because it makes it easier to understand how to behave in a given social situation. However, this can be harmful when it leads us to prioritize others' perceptions of our actions over our own. Our pursuit of status might drive us to make decisions that contradict our own desires and needs, simply because we believe it will grant us status in the eyes of others.

As explained, we cannot help but compare ourselves to others, using it as a means to understand ourselves and other people. We need it to mirror our actions in others', which helps us construct who we are and understand how to react in different situations. But we can also limit ourselves by defining a specific way of viewing life. We may not be able to avoid comparing ourselves, but we can work on better managing how we do it.

"Yes, that was great! But..."

One of the counterproductive effects of the comparison culture, as Baldwin and Mussweiler (2018) describe, can be termed the "but-trap". This happens, when we have taken actions that we are genuinely satisfied with, aligning with our deepest desires and needs. But then we compare ourselves to others. Suddenly, we are not so satisfied anymore.

This comparison culture can create a division in types of actions: those focusing on how we want others to perceive us, and those that we truly want to perform.

We constantly compare ourselves upwards, leading us to believe we are always lacking something. This affects the options we choose when making decisions. An example could be our career path, where we continue in a job because it maintains the image others have of us, even though it brings no joy. Our choice is based on what others should think of us, even though it might not cater to our own desires at all.

Conversely, we also choose some things because we truly want them. However, in a comparison culture focused on how we appear to others, we might over prioritize actions that cater to others' perception of us. For instance, you might love attending drama classes in your free time. But if these activities do not maintain the image you wish others to have of you, you might choose to keep it hidden. You compare yourself to your colleagues at work, who seemingly do not need activities that deviate from their work role, making you feel that you should not either.

How many people are afraid to show sides of themselves that don't support the person they believe they should be?

ONE'S TRUE SELF

In 1960, the renowned Scottish psychiatrist Ronald Laing published "The Divided Self—An Existential Study in Sanity and Madness." In this book he explores schizophrenia, adopting an existentialist perspective in his studies of the human psyche. Laing believed existential philosophy could be a tool in psychiatry to help people recover.

He describes schizophrenia as a reaction to the anxiety present in life, a novel viewpoint on this mental disorder at the time. His approach reflects existentialist thought, as he did not see schizophrenia as an irrational disturbance of the mind but rather a reaction to one's surroundings.

Laing made several intriguing discoveries in his studies of schizophrenia, which he linked strongly to the way we interact with others, especially how we understand ourselves through them. He explains that we create our self-understanding as we grow up. It is during this time that we develop our personality. We are not born with an identity or personality. We do not even know that our pain is uniquely our own.[57] Consider a baby crying when its parents leave the room. The baby does not yet understand that other people are unique individuals with their own thoughts. However, by expressing itself, for example by crying, it provokes a reaction from the parents. The fact that the child's action prompts a reaction slowly helps it understand that others are aware of its existence.

---

57   Laing, R. D. (2010). *The Divided Self—An Existential Study in Sanity and Madness.*

Laing suggests that this interplay between action and reaction helps develop our self-awareness as we grow. He particularly notes that parents who do not respond to their child's cries (or other actions) can contribute to the child becoming schizophrenic. According to Laing, the absence of a response leads the baby to believe that its actions cannot elicit a reaction, creating feelings of helplessness and confusion.

Recall Seligman's (1972) study on learned helplessness, which found that humans can convince themselves they are helpless. In their experiment involving a group of animals, all became passive when they believed they had no options after being subjected to unavoidable electric shocks. This understanding persisted, leading them to not take action for themselves later, even when they had the same opportunities as other animals in the experiment.

Both understandings highlight how we can become passive based on how others react to our actions. Laing demonstrated that children could develop feelings of helplessness and passivity if their parents did not respond to their actions during upbringing. Similarly, Seligman's study showed that animals in the experiment became passive when they believed they could do nothing, making themselves helpless.[58]

A divided personality

Laing argues that some individuals develop a dependency on reactions from others to feel part of the real world. Most of us have insecurities about certain aspects of ourselves, feeling inadequate in some way, whether it is about our appearance or social abilities. While having insecurities is normal, for a deeply insecure person, these feelings are much more profound. Such individuals face a dilemma in their social relationships. On one hand, they need other

---

58   Seligman, M. E. P. (1975). *Helplessness: On Depression, Development, and Death.*

people to feel alive, but on the other hand, it is these very people who can make them feel insecure.

Laing believes that many of us carry this understanding, which is similar to schizophrenia but still relatively normal. This is manifested when people divide their personality, feeling insecure and dealing with the dilemma created by their surroundings. He explains that people may create a false self to interact with their environment, displaying appropriate emotions in various social relations. However, this false self is a persona worn to hide the true self.

This concept of identity division can be applied across different activities in life. Think back to the last time you were in different social situations: a party, at work, and at your grandmother's house. How did you behave in each? Were you completely yourself in all situations, or did you act differently at the party with friends compared to being with your grandmother or at work? Most likely, there were variations in behavior.

We all engage in various social relations, each differing from our true self. It is natural to show different sides in different social contexts. However, it becomes problematic if we construct multiple false selves to fit into various situations, believing we should act a certain way at a party, work, or at our grandmother's. If these actions do not reflect our true personality, we end up maintaining a false self. Laing argues this can be incredibly damaging as we distance ourselves from our own thoughts, eventually becoming separated from ourselves and others.

We will no longer understand our own thoughts as we try to comprehend the person we think we should be, rather than who we truly are. This pattern emerges when we excessively try to understand ourselves through others. This perception can be traced back to our need for control, where through various false personas, we try to control our social relations. Believing that we need to behave in a certain way to fit in gives us a sense of control over our thoughts and others' perceptions of us.

BEING HAPPY AND HAVING CHOICES

Complications seem to be associated with our opportunities, although they are essential for living a happy and independent life. Political psychologist Robert Lane (2001) from Yale University points out that we face too many choices in life, and awareness of the potential overload on our psyche is needed. This is particularly crucial because we have not been provided with pre-set limitations to manage our options. Therefore, we risk accepting an identity given to us rather than seeing our identity as something to be discovered and crafted for ourselves.[59]

We may not be given the tools to handle our options, but ultimately it is up to us to navigate among them. As explained, more does not always mean better when it comes to the number of our options and the decisions we have to make.

But what is the ideal number of options? Can we imagine a "perfect number of options"? This question was explored by researchers in an experiment on consumer behavior, where they investigated the number of products to present to a person to maximize purchases. They used pens for the experiment and found that people bought the most when they were presented with 8-10 dif-

---

59   Lane, R. E. (2001). *The Loss of Happiness in Market Democracies.*

ferent pen options.[60] Unfortunately, this does not necessarily mean that 8-10 options are the answer to all life's big questions that will guarantee a happy life. However, it supports the idea that we can benefit from limiting the number of our many options if we are to be capable of taking action. After all, taking action and making decisions is how we exercise our freedom and realize ourselves, at least according to existentialist philosophy.

Expressing ourselves

Earlier in the book, you have read about Maslow's theory, which explains how we increasingly strive to realize ourselves through our actions. This is due to the fact that we have created greater welfare and more opportunities for the individual.[61]

Here, we seem to observe the same pattern when examining the motivation behind the choices and opportunities we pursue. Similarly, they also arise from a desire to express ourselves. Through our choices and opportunities, we are motivated to tell and show the world who we are. An example can be our clothing, where we dress based on how we want others to perceive us. You might want to be taken seriously by others, so you wear a suit to support the image you wish to present. Conversely, you may choose to dress differently to show others that you do not care about their opinions. Both are ways of self-realizing. You might prefer wearing a suit to pink leather pants, but the motivation behind your choices stems from the same desire to express yourself. You want to use your choices to show the world who you are.

However, the existentialist philosopher Jean-Paul Sartre would argue that our need to realize ourselves through superficial things supports a false understanding. He believes that through our clothing, we might conform to a direction defined as the objective truth

---

60 Shah, A. M. & Wolford, G. (2007). *Buying behavior as a function of parametric variation of number of choices.*

61 Maslow, A. (1943). *A Theory of Human Motivation*

by various authorities. In this case, one would be living a life in bad faith, imposing a role upon oneself and thereby not acting as a free individual.

In one of his works, he observes a waiter who has made it his identity to be a waiter.[62]As Sartre explains, the waiter cannot only be a waiter. He can be a human, he can be a man, but he cannot be defined solely by his profession. This fixed understanding contradicts the notion that humans are free. Instead, the waiter assigns himself a role, suggesting that he is meant to be a waiter. However, this goes against the philosophical concept that existence precedes essence.

Even though the waiter is proficient in his job and fully commits to his role, Sartre believes that he is merely playing the part of a waiter. By doing so, he also diminishes himself and his identity.[63] Comparing this to Laing's theory from the previous section, the waiter gives himself a false identity; a false self.

Sartre describes the waiter's movements as he serves guests at a café as being too precise and a bit too quick, while he speaks a bit too eagerly and appears a bit too accommodating. From an outside perspective, he would seem like the perfect waiter, whose primary purpose is to make the experience as pleasant as possible for his guests. However, Sartre believes that he has assumed the role of a waiter, which he tries to imitate as best as he can. Therefore, his movements are also fake and insincere, somewhat like a robot, as he describes in the book. The waiter's way of living out his role, in Sartre's eyes, is the same as eliminating his own individual person. Sartre believes that this pattern is repeated across numerous professions.[64]

---

62   Sartre, J. (1993). *Essays in Existentialism.*

63   Sartre, J. (2007). *Existentialism is a Humanism.*

64   Gosetti-Ferencei, J. (2021). *On Being and Becoming: An Existentialist Approach to Life An Existentialist Approach to Life.*

An example of this could be a doctor who steps into a role and starts speaking in a special way to his patients, because that is how a doctor should behave. Similarly, the doctor also tells himself that he must wear the right clothes because he is a doctor. The way we are perceived through our clothing seems to be justified on many points. For instance, there is a reason why our doctors wear a lab coat, as it is associated with our perception of the doctor's role.

In a survey involving 4,062 patients, 53% said that a doctor's clothing was very important to their perception of the care they received. Imagine if your own doctor walked into your first consultation wearing jogging clothes to inform you about your upcoming surgery. Most of us would probably not find it professional. We might even feel uneasy about this doctor performing our operation. But nothing has changed, except for the clothes the person is wearing. The person is still a doctor and possesses the same skills, whether dressed in jogging clothes or a lab coat.[65]

The way we dress acts as a means of expressing ourselves. However, according to existential philosophy, it can also contribute to maintaining a false identity that is not truly our own. Similarly, the choices we make become a symbol of our independence to the outside world. But at the same time, they can cause us to adhere to a set of actions that support an identity that does not necessarily originate from our own desires.

A desire for control

As you have read so far, it seems that we complicate our decision-making process. Instead of focusing on ourselves, we let others influence our choices. We compare ourselves to others and become dependent on their assessment of us, in order to create meaning in our decisions. Simultaneously, we try to find the best solution by

---

65 Petrilli, C. M., Saint, S. & Jennings, J. J., Caruso, A., Kuhn, L., Snyder, A., Chopra, V. (2018). *Understanding patient preference for physician attire: a cross-sectional observational study of 10 academic medical centres in the USA.*

weighing options and attempting to assign a value to all our possibilities. But this leads us to believe that there is a right and wrong when it comes to making choices.

Furthermore, it makes us believe that more choices also mean greater value, causing us to drown in an abundance of options and things we believe we must do. Our quest for the perfect choice leads us to react irrationally, where cognitive biases and other assumptions limit us. So, how do we ensure that we live a less complicated life—by making our decisions less complicated? And what are the consequences of not doing so?

Particularly the latter question is what the next part of the book will focus on. By examining some of the correlations between opportunities and mental health, we can better understand the consequences associated with how we handle our options. This serves as a rationale for why we should address the problem and rethink how we approach our opportunities, as well as how we handle the choices we make.

As you will read in the next part of the book, it seems that our mental well-being bears a weight because it has become more difficult to choose.

PART 5:
THE WEIGHT OF
OUR CHOICES

"It is difficult to find happiness within oneself,
but it is impossible to find it anywhere else."
–Arthur Schopenhauer

THE HAPPIEST COUNTRY
IN THE WORLD

Up to this point, we have explored the impact of our choices through both theoretical and philosophical lenses. Theoretically, modern consumer behavior studies have highlighted the difficulties we face in navigating and making decisions when presented with numerous options. These studies also show how this challenge can lead to psychological issues for individuals.

From a philosophical standpoint, existentialism encourages us to embrace our freedom and take action, while also highlighting how our approach to choices can foster anxiety and limit our understanding of our own freedom.

A pattern emerges, with both theoretical and philosophical insights pointing to the complications associated with the choices that come with our opportunities. Yet, it is clear that these choices are a byproduct of our freedom and welfare, suggesting that the issue is not the existence of these choices as such. Rather, it is about how we manage them, as they are essential for the expression of our freedom.

Despite these complexities associated with our choices, things generally seem to be going well in a Westernized country such as Denmark. The country has low unemployment, a high life expectancy, and sufficient food and shelter.

Denmark has even been named "the happiest country in the world" on multiple occasions. This designation comes from the

World Happiness Report, an annual survey that ranks global happiness. In determining a country's happiness, the organization considers various data points such as average life expectancy, income, etc. Additionally, their evaluation process includes questionnaires asking individuals about their sense of freedom to make important life decisions. [66] [67]

The ability to choose plays a crucial role in the World Happiness Report's evaluation of countries' happiness levels. However, the report primarily investigates whether individuals feel they have the freedom to make important life decisions. It does not address the mental consequences associated with making these choices, which is an intriguing aspect to explore further in understanding Denmark's happiness.

Mental illness in Denmark

Despite Denmark's title as the happiest country in the world, a different picture emerges when examining the rise of mental illness. A report by the Danish Psychiatry Foundation (2021) estimates that one in three Danes will experience a mental illness at some point in their lives. That is a significant portion of the population. Upon reading these figures, it is upsetting to consider that 33% of Danes are expected to suffer from a mental illness. How does this align with being one of the happiest countries in the world?

According to the Danish Psychiatry Foundation's report, approximately 700,000 adults in Denmark experience symptoms of mental illness annually. Anxiety disorders are the most common among adults. However, it is especially concerning for children and young people, as early onset of mental illness can have lasting negative impacts on their lives. Thankfully, many people recover from mental illnesses, although they might experience multiple episodes throughout their life. The report further reveals that about

---

66   Danmarks Statistik (2021). M

67   World Happiness Report (2021)

10% of the Danish population will be affected by depression at some point, 1.3% are expected to develop substance or alcohol dependence, and 0.8% will suffer from anxiety. When compared with other EU countries, Denmark has the highest incidence of anxiety disorders.

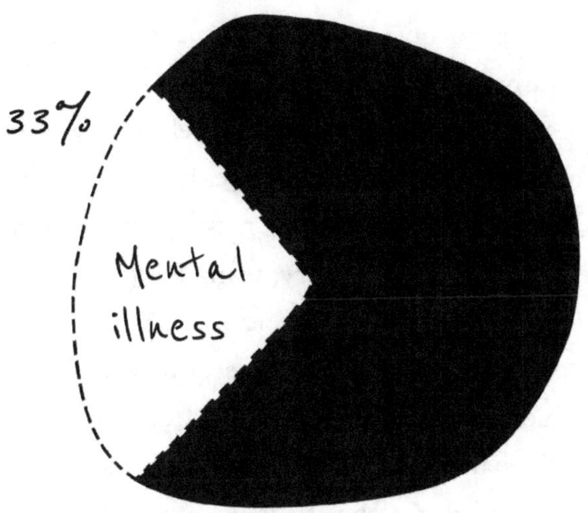

Delving deeper into the report's data, it is evident that the majority of individuals suffering from either anxiety or depression belong to the country's labor force. Approximately 70% of those with depression and 65% of those with anxiety are employed.

Yet, in 2015, Denmark spent 5.4% of its GDP on expenses related to mental illness, amounting to about 110 billion DKK. The report also indicates that around 60% of young people aged 18-29 with a mental illness are either in education or employed. Furthermore, mental illness is identified as one of the primary reasons young people struggle to complete their education. This situation suggests that young people do not have the most favorable conditions to successfully pursue their studies. It also highlights the urgency of addressing the issues of mental illness and well-being.[68]

---

68   Psykiatrifonden (2021). *Tal og fakta om psykisk sygdom i Danmark.*

Do we remember our freedom?

While Denmark may be on top of the list of the "world's happiest countries," there is a rising number of Danes diagnosed with mental illnesses. Conditions like anxiety and depression seem closely linked to the same complications observed in consumer behavior studies, focusing on how we handle our choices, especially when faced with numerous options.

The question arises: are we effectively utilizing our freedom without constraints? Or does the increase in mental illness, suffering, and discontent stem from not making choices that align with our desires and should, in theory, bring happiness? Are we falling into the trap of doing what we believe others think we should do? If so, we might not associate our freedom with being truly free, feeling unable to make choices that reflect our true desires. The danger here is that an abundance of choices may contribute to the negative trend in mental health issues, fundamentally caused by the increasing complexity of decision-making and defining our own path in life.

As discussed in the previous section of the book, various studies demonstrate how our choices—and lack thereof—can affect us. The following sections will delve into psychological studies that mirror earlier discussions about consumer behavior. They touch on several aspects of human psychology, each elucidating how we approach the opportunities we encounter.

What does it mean to be happy?

Do you know what makes you happy? It is a difficult question to answer, as there is no definitive response. If you ask the existentialist movement, anything can make you happy, but it requires you first to convince yourself of such.

Jean-Paul Sartre put it this way:

> "Life has no meaning a priori… It is up to you to give
> it a meaning, and value is nothing but the meaning
> that you choose."[69]

In other words, we can only find joy in our actions if we are the ones creating it. However, numerous psychological studies suggest that certain things can indeed influence our sense of happiness. Examining these in relation to existentialism allows us to explore the concept of happiness from both a theoretical and philosophical perspective. Applying both aspects can be beneficial in understanding and achieving happiness.

Philosophically, it is emphasized that we must take action to create joy and meaning in our lives. But in a world full of choices, studies in consumer behavior have also shown that we find decision-making more challenging. Believing that the ultimate answer or perfect opportunity is just around the corner, we analyze and evaluate all presented options.

But as existentialism explains, there are no right or wrong choices. There are only the choices you make yourself.

"The crucial thing is to find a truth which is truth for me, to find the idea for which I am willing to live and die." as Kierkegaard put it in one of his essays.[70] Only if your actions are rooted in your own desires and what you associate with happiness will you find meaning.

But it is not just philosophy that advises us to find answers within ourselves. Recent research in human psychology supports this sentiment. Michael Robinson and Michael Eid (2017) compiled several significant studies on the mental processes associated

---

69   Sartre, J. (2007). *Existentialism is a Humanism.*

70   Pattison, G. (2013). *Kierkegaard and the Quest for Unambiguous Life: Between Romanticism and Modernism: Selected Essays.*

with our sense of joy and well-being. They describe various cognitive processes that can impact us either positively or negatively. Several of the most relevant will be reviewed in the following sections, supplemented with additional research to help unveil what it means to be happy.[71]

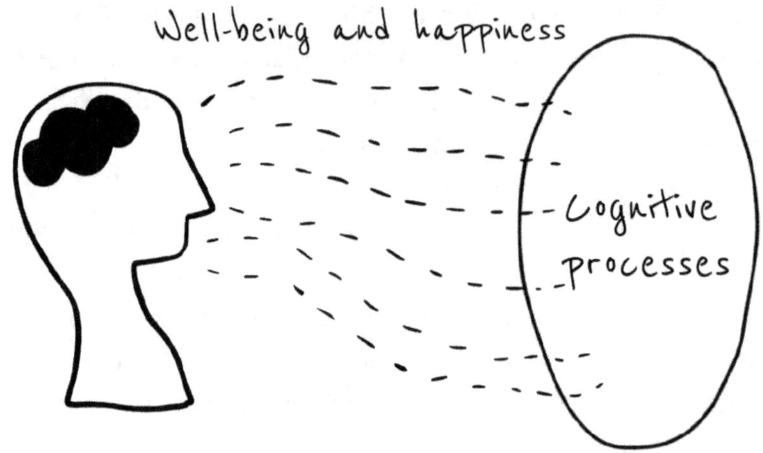

Optimism

A crucial cognitive process linked to happiness is our ability to focus and maintain an optimistic outlook. This follows the notion that our mind chooses what to focus on and, thus, determining what influences our well-being.

This focus can be on either positive or negative information. To be happy, we ideally need to concentrate on the positive aspects of life. Whether the information that occupies our thoughts is positive or negative depends on whether we are optimistic or pessimistic. Research shows that optimistic individuals tend to focus more on positive impressions from their surroundings, which fosters joy. Other studies have also indicated that people generally experience greater life satisfaction when they maintain an optimistic attitude.

---

71   Robinson, M. & Eid, M. (2017). *Introduction to the Happy Mind: Cognitive Contributions to Well-Being.*

In fact, some researchers believe that we can teach ourselves to be optimistic, particularly by focusing on what we have rather than what we lack. By doing this, we concentrate on the positive events in our lives instead of fixating on our deficiencies and, consequently, on things that don't happen for us.[72]

"If only I had their life," you might think while looking at others' fantastic vacation photos, as you read the morning newspaper at your local café, sipping coffee made with beans from Central America and nibbling on a freshly baked morning bun. Everything is relative. The way we relate to what we have—and do not have—can have more significant consequences than we might realize, especially when it leads us to neglect what we do have.

We have the ability to influence whether we approach our past, present, and future with optimism or pessimism. Researchers have identified that those who are optimistic are better at acknowledging if they have a problem. They do not deny it if they could have done something better in the past or if they are facing a challenge. Instead, they try to be proactive in finding solutions and moving forward.[73]

In today's world, it is important for us to actively engage with the mental challenges that arise from having to make choices among the many options available to us. Recognizing these challenges, instead of ignoring them, can assist us in staying forward-thinking and optimistic about the choices we have.

The Hedonic Treadmill

Another mental process associated with happiness is our ability to adapt to our circumstances. In short, to become accustomed to what we have. Interestingly, when something bad happens in

---

72   Wadlinger, H. A. & Isaacowitz, D. M (2011). *Fixing our focus: Training attention to regulate emotion.*

73   Segerstrom, S. C. (2007). *Optimism and resources: Effects on each other and on health over 10 years.*

our lives, it can have a positive effect. Conversely, when we experience good things, it can actually have a negative effect. We get used to the level of goodness in our lives, which causes us to neglect its value. This phenomenon is described in the following as 'The Hedonic Treadmill', a term introduced by Brickman and Campbell in 1971. The word hedonism, which forms the basis of this concept, means to see pleasure as a purpose in life.[74][75]

The Hedonic Treadmill explains humanity's constant pursuit of more pleasure. When we relate this to how we adapt to our circumstances, it manifests through a variety of our actions. For instance, it is evident in the way our consumption increases as our income grows.[76]

As a result, we create a spiral where we earn more and spend more. In the concept of The Hedonic Treadmill this is described as constantly running after more but not actually moving forward.

The treadmill might move faster, but we remain in the same place. In modern society, this development of our needs is not hard to spot. However, psychological research has shown that the quantity of our positive experiences weighs more heavily than material goods when assessing our happiness. We might not have been able to afford expensive items when we were students, but we could certainly create good experiences. And often, these experiences have a greater impact on whether we are happy or not, the studies suggest.

Inspiration

When we feel inspired, it is typically associated with a sense of joy. Studies have also shown that inspiration promotes creativity,

---

74   Brickman, P., & Campbell, D. T. (1971). *Hedonic relativism and planning the good society.* In M. H. Appley (Ed.), Adaptation-level theory. New York: Academic Press.

75   Frederick, S. & Loewenstein, G. (1999). *Hedonic adaptation.*

76   Parkinson, C. N. (1996). *Parkinson's law.*

a mental state linked with happiness and well-being. In moments of inspiration, we often take more actions based on our intuition rather than our rationale.[77] And as previously explained, we experience greater joy when we can act intuitively without overthinking.

If you have a hobby which you are passionate about, you might be familiar with this feeling. Maybe you enjoy painting and always find that time flies when you are engaged in this activity. You are in a creative zone, not thinking about what you are doing—you are just doing it. Your intuition takes over, and you express yourself creatively. In that moment, you are inspired, which, according to several studies, contributes to creating happiness and well-being. However, we cannot expect to be inspired all the time, so it is important to challenge ourselves with new projects. This way, we can increase the frequency of those moments when we feel inspired, as they do not always occur spontaneously.

Positive thoughts

It may seem obvious, but our happiness is closely linked to positive thoughts. Researchers have examined how positive thoughts can expand our attention to more positive things. In fact, maintaining a positive outlook can have an amplifying effect on our entire life. Barbara Fredrickson (2001) developed the *broaden-and-build* theory, which explains that one positive thought is more likely to generate another positive thought.

Thus, a snowball of positive thoughts can gradually grow larger and larger. However, it primarily involves staying curious, creative, and experimental, as these are linked to positive thoughts. The broaden-and-build theory builds upon some of the previously described cognitive processes, such as being inspired and optimistic.[78]

Research also shows that we are less stressed when we have positive thoughts, and this makes us more present in social interac-

---

77   Thrash, T. M., Elliot, A. J. (2003). *Inspiration as a psychological construct.*

78   Fredrickson, B. L. (2001). *The role of positive emotions in positive psychology.*

tions.[79] [80] Contrary to positive thoughts, negative thoughts limit our actions and prevent us from benefiting from the positive aspects associated with our positive thoughts. This means that if you can identify the things that spark your curiosity, you can initiate the same self-reinforcing process. In terms of your options, it is therefore advantageous to remain curious and make choices that ignite your enthusiasm. But this requires first focusing on yourself, after which you can associate your choices with positive value.

Meaning

It may seem impossible to give a definitive answer to what it means to be happy. Yet, several studies show that one of the most significant positive impacts on our happiness occurs when we find meaning in what we do. For some, the answer may seem obvious; life needs to have meaning for us to be happy. Typically, this is easier said than done. Therefore, exploring what it means for us to create meaning is interesting when trying to understand what it means to be happy.

Research has shown that meaning is a crucial element for our well-being. People who describe having a clear purpose in their life also rate themselves as happier than those who do not have a sense of purpose.[81]

In an experiment, it was demonstrated that while philosophy can be a tool to understand what it means to experience meaning in life, meaning is not created until one takes action. Instead, it was shown that people who follow their intuition find it easier to create meaning. Especially those who are more guided by their impulses

---

79   Fredrickson, B. L. & Levenson, R. W. (1998). *Positive emotions speed recovery from the cardiovascular sequelae of negative emotions.*

80   Waugh C. E. & Fredrickson, B. L. (2006). *Nice to know you: Positive emotions, self-other overlap, and complex understanding in the formation of a new relationship.*

81   Heintzelman, S. J. & King, L. A. (2014). *Life is pretty meaningful.*

without always rationalizing everything are better at finding meaning in their actions and in their life.[82]

This line of thinking aligns with existentialist philosophy, which advocates for taking action. It is through action that one can create meaning in life, as life does not come with a predetermined meaning. You must create your own meaning. The studies indicate there might be some truth in this. Perhaps we should think a little less when making our decisions.

Control

Feeling in control has also been shown to be significant for our sense of happiness. Researchers have found a correlation between our feeling of control and overall joy in life.[83]

In a world full of choices, this is reflected in many of our actions. As described in the first part of the book, we attempt to control our options through various consumption patterns. For instance, we try to minimize the number of choices to feel more comfortable with the decisions we make. At the same time, we cannot help but research everything we can about the things we are about to purchase. We strive to create a sense of control, which also appears to be linked to our ability to be happy.

But what happens when the number of our options increases, and we still try to maintain a sense of control? According to behavioral science studies, we tend to feel increasingly uncomfortable when faced with too many choices. And in the existentialist movement, the Danish philosopher Søren Kierkegaard describes it as feeling anxiety over the multitude of opportunities freedom offers.

I believe that our need for control presents a risk for modern humans. When faced with an increasing number of options, we may

---

82 King, L. A., Hicks, J. A., Krull, J. L. & Del Gaiso, A. K. (2006). *Positive affect and the experience of meaning in life.*

83 Lachman, M. E. (2006). *Perceived control over aging-related declines: Adaptive beliefs and behaviors.*

try to maintain a sense of control. But as the number increases, it becomes harder.

I think that we build our own bubble of control in an effort to limit and avoid making too many decisions. We start to develop habits and routines that help us not to face every decision. This has both advantages and disadvantages, as I see it. The advantage is that it minimizes the number of our options, giving us more mental energy to use on things that are valuable to us.

For example, we might eat the same food and wear the same clothes to avoid constantly making choices that do not create lasting value for us. The disadvantage arises if we start to shield ourselves from new things that extend beyond our habits. When that happens, we lose our optimism and instead see our options as something dangerous trying to disrupt our control bubble. In such cases, we might ask ourselves whether our desire to feel in control actually leads to losing control?

According to studies, there can be several forms of control, but particularly two perceptions matter most: primary and secondary control.

We can either have primary control, referring to whether we feel we can influence our surroundings, or secondary control, focusing on whether we feel we can adapt to challenges from our environment. Those with a low sense of primary control are more dependent on secondary control to feel happy. Thus, we generally prefer to feel that we can influence our surroundings. And when we cannot, we try to adapt. However, adapting also has a negative impact on our happiness. Research, therefore, tells us that it is beneficial to feel that we can influence our surroundings, as it seems to positively contribute to our overall well-being.[84]

While we do not always have influence over how our surroundings evolve, resistance can arise where we cannot always affect the

---

84   Heckhausen, J. & Schulz, R. (1995). *A life-span theory of control.*

outcome of a particular situation, leading to secondary control. However, existentialism suggests that we can limit the effect of secondary control, especially by not letting our lives be governed by other authorities. This does not imply that we should avoid following any form of authority, as Sartre discusses in his view of existentialism.

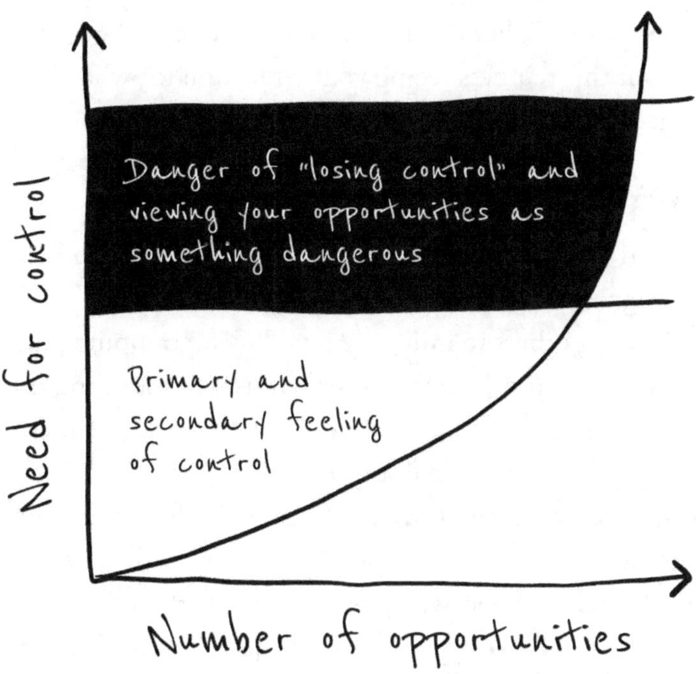

Let me give you an example. You have started a higher education program where you must follow a set of guidelines defined by the university. This would be the authority Sartre speaks of. Here, you can fall into the trap of seeing yourself as lacking control over your actions and therefore resorting to secondary control. You tell yourself that you do not have primary control, but instead, you need to adapt to the challenging environment of education. In this case, you are being controlled by an authority instead of believing that you can influence your surroundings. Doing so creates a sense of control, which in turn generates happiness. Existentialism suggests that this is achieved through your actions.

Does this mean you should avoid all authority to be happy? Of course not. But you can reflect on the value you assign to authority. If not, you risk seeing yourself as being without control. You may tell yourself that you cannot influence your surroundings, but instead, you must accept them as part of your life. However, as in the example with higher education, one could also choose to simply stop. But this requires seeing your education for what it is—an opportunity.

Comparison

As described in earlier sections of the book, our need to compare ourselves significantly influences how we make decisions. We can end up allowing others to influence our choices, trapping ourselves in a pursuit of what others have—or tell us what we should have. When considering what affects our happiness, our tendency to compare ourselves plays a major role.

Several studies suggest that our overall life satisfaction depends on social comparison. Generally, they show that we feel better about ourselves when we appear better off than other people. Conversely, we feel worse when others seem to be doing better than us. Therefore, our ability to be happy is dependent on how we compare ourselves to others and the implications this has for our self-perception.[85]

The frequency and depth of comparing ourselves to others differ from person to person. However, researchers believe that there are two general ways of comparing oneself with others: either by identifying with another person or by differentiating oneself from another person. The former is based on what we have in common, while the latter focuses on our differences.

---

85   Gibbons, F. X. & Buunk, B. P. (1999). *Individual differences in social comparison: Development of a scale of social comparison orientation.*

When we compare ourselves to someone and we identity with them, it can create a feeling of well-being if that person is doing well. Conversely, if the person is doing poorly, we might feel bad about ourselves. We understand the person's pain because we identify ourselves with them. This can happen, for example, when you feel happy for a friend who gets a new job. You feel glad on your friend's behalf because you understand and can identify with her.

On the other hand, when we differentiate ourselves from someone else, the opposite happens. We feel better about ourselves when the person is doing poorly, while we feel worse about ourselves when the person is doing well.[86]

In our society, the urge to set ourselves apart from others is apparent in various situations. For example, when a famous person encounters problems that are communicated to the public, many of us are drawn to follow the story, absorbing all the gossip available. Since the person is famous, it becomes easier for us to keep up with their life, thus simplifying the task of comparing ourselves to them. When they start having troubles, we become more curious and often feel better about our own lives. This occurs because we compare ourselves with the individual, but do not feel a connection to them. If they are struggling, we tend to feel more satisfied with ourselves. We might not like to admit it, but psychological studies indicate this is a normal part of how we compare ourselves to others.

Social comparison, motivated by the desire to distinguish oneself from someone else, comes with several drawbacks. Most notably, it makes us dependent on others for our happiness, especially when it is tied to their lack of success. Existentialism teaches that we should concentrate on ourselves and not seek validation from others. When we compare ourselves to others, we shift our focus

---

86   Buunk, B. P. & Ybema, J. F. (1997). *Social comparisons and occupational stress: The identification-contrast model.*

away from ourselves, but in the end, it is only ourselves that can create our own happiness.

Jean-Paul Sartre, an existentialist philosopher, believed that we all need social relationships. Not necessarily because we like the people with whom we interact but because of how these people make us feel.

When we compare this idea with the motivation behind our relationships, as explained in the previous theory about human psychology, there are clear parallels. In that theory, it is emphasized that we are more inclined to accept people with whom we can identify. This concept closely aligns with Sartre's thoughts. Could it be that our motives for self-fulfillment are what drive our social interactions?

If we accept this, we should then consider who we spend our time with and whether these individuals genuinely have our best interests at heart. We should also reflect on whether we genuinely wish well for the people in our lives. If not, it might be that we keep them around primarily because of their ability to help us maintain a certain image.

Using others as a tool to maintain a certain image leads to a deviation from our true selves, making us reliant on others. Furthermore, philosophy suggests that it is inauthentic to compare oneself to others, as it shifts focus from our own identity. It can also be argued that a healthy and balanced life should not include wishing to see others struggle. Seeking joy in the troubles of others leaves us surrounded by negativity and pessimism.

But what about people we do not know and cannot relate to? Research suggests that we can bring more joy into our lives by learning to relate to other people, rather than distancing ourselves from them. It is worth considering how we compare ourselves to others.

Have you thought about whether you identify with others and feel happy when they succeed or do you separate yourself from them, feeling better when they have difficulties?

Studies in human psychology can help us better understand what brings us happiness. However, they cannot tell us exactly how to be happy. They can offer guidelines, just like existentialist philosophy. Neither one nor another can provide a strict guide for a happy life full of joy, as happiness is always subjective. But by combining research with existentialist philosophy, we can make these concepts more concrete. We can develop perspectives that help us understand what might bring us happiness. Then, it is up to us to act, as existentialism suggests. Only then can we determine if our choices bring us value and happiness.

FINDING HAPPINESS IN OUR ACTIONS

Do you ever feel like your days are all the same? Maybe you sense that each day begins in a similar fashion: you wake up, you eat breakfast, you get ready, and you head to work. Then a day filled with a series of decisions awaits, each demanding action from you. And when the day ends, you can look forward to doing it all over again tomorrow.

Our days often appear monotonous when we take moments to reflect on our routines. Even when we become aware of these thoughts, we carry on. When the next day dawns, we rise, we prepare, and we start our daily tasks again. This is what existentialist philosophy would define as the absurdity of life. Here, it is up to an individual to define their own life. Meaning is not preordained; it must be created by oneself.

Can it be that we also can seek meaning in the midst of repetitive days? Despite this feeling, it seems we are influenced by something greater that keeps us going. But what exactly is it that motivates us?

Many might be inclined to answer that money is the motivation behind our actions. It is no secret that money plays a significant role in the world, often associated with a sense of freedom. However, research shows that money actually plays a lesser role than many of us might think.

In reality, what motivates us is made up of complex processes. We are motivated by a wide range of things, many of which are subjective, making it impossible to present a one-size-fits-all solution. However, research can again guide us in understanding what motivates us. As described in the previous section of the book, our ability to create meaning in our actions is crucial for happiness. The same applies to our ability to stay motivated and get up every single day without viewing the repetition of many of the same actions as negative.

Understanding what actions make us happy is one thing, but it's even more important to figure out how to find meaning in those actions.

Professor Dan Ariely (2016) from Duke University has conducted research into what motivates us. In one of his studies, he explored this through an experiment involving LEGO.[87]

He asked a group of participants to build special figures out of LEGO bricks. One half of the test group generally found the activity exciting and cared about the figures they built. The other half, however, found the exercise boring and did not care much about their figures. After both groups had assembled their figures, they were all disassembled in front of the participants, who were then asked to build new LEGO figures. By disassembling the figures while the participants watched, many became demotivated, which was the intention of the experiment. After a few rounds, none of the participants wanted to continue. Not even those who had enjoyed the exercise and liked assembling the figures. Ariely believed that because the participants could not see any meaning in their action, neither the engaged nor the disengaged participants wanted to continue.

To investigate further, he conducted another experiment. Again, participants were asked to assemble LEGO figures, but this

---

87   Ariely, D. (2016). *Payoff: The Hidden Logic That Shapes Our Motivations.*

time the figures were not disassembled afterward. Instead, participants were asked to build a new figure in addition to the one they already made. As a result, they became less demotivated because they could see more meaning in their actions. However, the disengaged participants stopped again after just a few rounds, while the engaged ones continued for significantly longer. According to Ariely, the experiment showed that regardless of whether you like an activity or not, you will lose motivation if you cannot see the meaning in what you are doing.

In relation to the choices you face, you must be able to find meaning in the decisions you make. If you cannot, your days will come to feel monotonous, and you will feel demotivated. But as you will read in the following, we can come to believe that certain things will make us happy, even though reality may be different.

Money and happiness

Imagine that you won so much money that you could do whatever you wanted for the rest of your life. Money would no longer be a concern for you. For many, this seems like the epitome of being free and happy. However, research shows that people who win the lottery generally return to their original level of happiness after just one year. That means even if you win $100 million today, you can expect to be as happy a year from now as you are right now.

This reminds us that more options are not always associated with being happier. In many cases, the opposite occurs when the number of options becomes too large.

In a study by Daniel Kahneman and Angus Deaton (2010) involving over 450,000 participants, the relationship between money and happiness was examined. The study found that there was a correlation between the amount of money and happiness, but only up to a certain limit.

It turned out that money only created more happiness for the participants up to an income of about $75.000 a year. Those who earned more were not necessarily happier. The study thus shows that we do not become happier by earning more after a certain limit. So, whether you earn $5.000.000 or $75.000 a year, does not significantly impact your happiness.

Instead, a stronger sense of happiness is associated with our social relationships. The same study showed that those who had people in their lives whom they liked were also happier. This means that people who are married, have good friends, are close with their family, or are part of a larger community have a greater chance of being happy with their lives. Social relationships were more important than money to the participants when assessing how happy they were.

According to Kevin Horsley and Louis Fourie (2018), we, as humans, have become accustomed to tying our happiness to things that extend beyond ourselves as the world has become more complex.[88] In their research, they explain that we increasingly associate our happiness with moments of fleeting joy.

As a result, we link the right car, the right clothes, the right job, the right house, the right vacation, the right partner, or a special achievement with the feeling of being happy. However, these things often only provide us with brief feelings of joy, leading us to constantly seek more. Consequently, we become dependent on external things for our happiness.

In another study, Liad Bareket-Bojmel, Guy Hochman, and Dan Ariely (2013) examined the relationship between money and motivation among employees at the American company Intel.[89]

The researchers offered a bonus to the employees responsible for assembling the company's computer chips if they could assemble a certain amount. After initiating the experiment, the re-

---

88   Horsley, K. & Fourie, L. (2018). *The Happy Mind: A Simple Guide to Living a Happier Life Starting Today.*

89   Bareket-Bojmel, L., Hochman, G. & Ariely, D. (2014). *It's (Not) All About the Jacksons: Testing Different Types of Short-Term Bonuses in the Field*

searchers observed a positive effect on the employees' productivity. However, this increased productivity lasted only for a single day. The next day, their production level dropped again. It seemed that the money only created a temporary motivation for the employees.

To explore what else could influence the employees' productivity, the researchers tried a different approach. If the employees did well and managed to assemble a specific number of computer chips, they were told that they would receive a message at the end of the day. The message stated that they had done a good job and that their boss appreciated their effort.

It turned out that this message was more effective in improving results over several days compared to the money-based bonus. From this, the researchers could show that people are more motivated by compliments and internal motivation factors rather than money and external motivation factors. They believed that an internal motivation factor worked over a longer period because the employees could take ownership of their work. They were not required to reach a certain quantity of computer chips to assemble. Instead, they could choose to do so if they wanted to be recognized for their work.

It appears that money does not have the desired effect on our happiness as we often believe. If we focus on other things instead, such as taking ownership of our actions and maintaining strong social relationships, we seem to be able to give ourselves a better starting point to find meaning in our actions and create greater happiness in life.

Midlife crisis

A midlife crisis typically occurs when one is between 40 and 65 years old, although it can certainly happen earlier or later in life. It is challenging to precisely define what constitutes a midlife crisis, and as such, there is no concrete data to indicate how many people experience it. This phenomenon often manifests as a sudden urge to change one's life, accompanied by existential questioning and reevaluation of one's past decisions and current trajectory.

American philosophy professor Kieran Setiya (2017) delves into this topic, exploring what it means to go through a midlife crisis. Most of us are familiar with the term, and some might associate it with stereotypes like the family man suddenly withdrawing his savings, purchasing a new car, and leaving with a younger partner.

Setiya himself experienced a midlife crisis, sparking his interest in the subject as he struggled to understand why he suddenly doubted who he had become or questioned his past actions. Despite being a successful professor at the prestigious Massachusetts Institute of Technology (MIT) and having a good family life, he found himself contemplating what more he could desire.

The midlife crisis arises, in part, from reflecting on our past and wondering about the "roads not taken" or pondering how life might have been different had we made alternate choices.

It is often a challenge to appreciate our current lives without overthinking the past. Some might argue that it is an art to value one's present life without dwelling too much on what has been.

This period of introspection and doubt can lead to significant life changes, as individuals seek to align their current lives with their values, desires, and aspirations.[90] Questions like "Have I achieved what I wanted?", "Have I made the right choices?", and "Is there more to life?" often arise during a midlife crisis. According to Kieran Setiya, it is common for most people to experience a midlife crisis at some point. While not everyone may withdraw their savings to buy a new car or leave with a younger partner, many start to question their existence as they grow older and gradually come to terms with their mortality. Setiya argues that it is a natural part of life to question the decisions one has made, especially noting that a midlife crisis can be a delayed response to choices made in one's late 20s or early 30s.

---

90   Setiya, K. (2017). *Midlife: A Philosophical Guide.*

The crisis is often associated with a sense of emptiness, as if one's past choices and actions lose their value due to these doubts.

Carl Jung, a Swiss psychiatrist, was among the first to describe the concept of a midlife crisis. He regarded it as a period when individuals feel compelled to evaluate their life and explore their psyche. Jung also perceived it as a time that demands letting go of the ego and contemplating existential aspects of life. This period of reevaluation and introspection can be both challenging and transformative, leading to significant personal growth and a deeper understanding of oneself and one's place in the world.[91] Many of us might find it daunting to delve into the depths of our minds and question the grand aspects of life. However, failing to pause and reflect on our lives can lead to an inauthentic existence, according to existentialist philosophy. The stereotypical image of a midlife crisis, like the family man suddenly driving around in a new sports car, might seem somewhat inauthentic as well.

Kieran Setiya suggests that we should become better at embracing our mistakes which is an idea that is supported by existentialism.

Life is full of difficult decisions, and trying to find the best solution by overanalyzing and weighing all alternatives against each other is not always helpful. Sometimes, it is better to just make a decision, even if it leads to mistakes. Embracing these errors is preferable to not doing anything.

We cannot all become movie stars, even if that was our dream. Therefore, we should not view our opportunities as deficiencies in our current lives but as signs of all the good things in life in general.

There are ways to make life easier for ourselves. Firstly, we can turn to philosophy and reflect on death.

Death can be used as a tool to decide how we want to live our lives and to find peace in our actions, learning to enjoy the process associated with our choices rather than focusing solely on the

---

91   Dirda, M. (2010). *Jung and the midlife crisis.*

outcomes. Setiya explains that we can also become better at setting goals by understanding the difference between what he defines as *telic* and *atelic* goals.

Telic goals are result-focused activities that always have an end and often leave us feeling unsatisfied once they are achieved. These include tasks like paying bills, cleaning, or quickly preparing dinner for the family—actions that do not leave us feeling particularly fulfilled.

Atelic goals, on the other hand, are based on activities that have no end and seem to be more meaningful to us. These are experienced when spending time with family and friends, listening to music, or engaging in projects that make a difference. Setiya argues that we should set more atelic goals, as the actions performed in pursuit of these goals are less likely to be associated with the regret often seen in people experiencing a midlife crisis.

The recurring theme in a midlife crisis is the doubt we cast on the choices we have made, similar to the phenomenon observed in consumer behavior studies. This is exemplified by the jam experiment mentioned earlier in the book, where participants were more likely to regret their choice when faced with selecting from 24 types of jam instead of just six.

This parallels our life decisions, where we struggle to see the larger meaning in our past actions. Looking back, everything seems clearer with hindsight, making us wonder if we should have chosen to become a rockstar and travel the world instead of pursuing our current career. But reality is different. Without pausing occasionally to reflect, we cannot appreciate our actions—both those which we have taken in the past and those which we are taking now.

Studying the reasons behind midlife crises can teach us a lot about making choices. These crises seem to be driven by similar factors that influence our consumer behavior, especially the tendency to dwell on past choices, allowing them to negatively impact our present lives. We reminisce about how life could have been better, which hampers our ability to find meaning in our current actions.

Imagine you are part of the jam experiment. Instead of enjoying the strawberry jam, which you have chosen, you cannot help but wonder if the blackcurrant jam might have tasted better. This leads you to overlook the goodness of the strawberry jam in front of you.

Perfectionism

There appears to be a link between the number of options available to us and an increased pressure to always make the right choices. This is particularly evident in how we scrutinize the consequences of our decisions, especially when considering what we might miss out on if our actions are not executed perfectly. This issue is becoming increasingly widespread, particularly among younger people.

A study involving 40,000 students from the United Kingdom, the United States, and Canada, spanning from 1989 to 2016, revealed that perfectionism is a growing problem among the youth, potentially leading to various mental health issues such as anxiety and depression.

The study also highlighted that young people have particularly high self-expectations in social contexts. In fact, this was one of the highest-scoring factors in terms of their self-imposed expectations. The correlation between this type of expectation and serious mental health conditions like anxiety, depression, and suicidal thoughts is a significant cause for concern. This suggests a need for greater awareness and strategies to help young people manage these high self-expectations and the pursuit of perfectionism.[92]

---

92   Curran, T. & Hill, A. P. (2019). *Perfectionism Is Increasing Over Time: A Meta-Analysis of Birth Cohort Differences From 1989 to 2016.*

"According to the World Health Organization (WHO), we have never seen such a high number of young people suffering from mental illnesses like anxiety and depression."[93]

While it is challenging to directly link these issues to the increase in choices available, researchers believe there is a correlation between rising perfectionism and mental health issues among the youth. As options multiply, so does the pressure to make the "right" choices, as discussed in the first chapter of the book. The impact of increased perfectionism cannot be overlooked.

However, some researchers argue that the problem is not the abundance of choices, but rather a generation that is spoiled and overly sensitive. This perspective views the younger generation, particularly those born between 1980-1994, known as the snowflake generation, as the reason why choices are perceived as problematic. Whether the issue lies with the individuals or the inherent pressure of making the right choices is subject to personal interpretation. It is important to note that the world was different before the 1980s, with fewer opportunities and consequently, different expectations.

Despite this, the current situation appears to have serious repercussions, especially evident in the youth's need for perfection. Research indicates that young people set irrational and sometimes unattainable goals, believing they must achieve everything. This leads to unrealistic self-expectations, affecting academic performance, the desire for material possessions, and even changes in physical appearance.[94]

---

93   World Health Organization (2017). *Depression and Other Common Mental Disorders. Global Health Estimates.*

94   Curran, T. & Hill, A. P.(2018). *Perfectionism Is Increasing, and That's Not Good News.*

A Harvard Business Review article from 2018 highlights a concerning trend among young people: the creation of a myth that everything connected to their choices must be perfect.

This perception places immense pressure on individuals, especially in a world brimming with options. A natural reaction to this abundance of choices is an attempt to maintain control to ensure perfection. However, the combination of increasing options and a surge in perfectionism can be a dangerous mix, potentially leading to mental health issues.

The article emphasizes that perfectionism is an unattainable goal. In striving for it, individuals become dependent on the approval of others and set themselves up for failure since everyone ultimately makes mistakes. This pursuit of perfectionism can lead to self-doubt, anxiety, and even feelings of shame. It is important to teach young people that striving to be perfect is unhealthy and that having flaws is not a sign of weakness.

Educational institutions, facing increased pressure on students, should advocate that sometimes "good enough" is better than perfect. They could adopt Herbert Simon's satisficing principle, which suggests saving mental energy by accepting that one's actions and results are satisfactory, rather than striving for perfection.

However, implementing this mindset is easier said than done. One of the main reasons for the rise in the pursuit of perfection among youth and people, in general, may stem from a lack of curiosity about why we make our decisions. The study emphasizes that students should be satisfied with good enough and not seek perfection. But in a context where, for instance, pursuing studies in fields like architecture, journalism, or international trade requires near-perfect grades, it is challenging for young people to aim for anything less than perfection.* This situation creates a paradox where the demands of the educational system conflict with the mental well-being of its students.[95]

If the goal can only be achieved through perfection, it might seem a bit simplistic to say that we should just get used to saying, 'okay is good enough.' If one is passionate about something, is not it okay to do it as well as one can? In that case, one remains true to oneself and one's values, and it is surely not bad for well-being and happiness to want to explore and perfect one's passion.

But the problem arises when one chases something that, in reality, is not something one truly desires. Here, existentialist philosophy can guide us by reminding us that none of our actions have any significance to anyone but ourselves. In the grand scheme of things, it is actually irrelevant.

I do not believe that the problem of perfectionism is limited to young students, but that it increasingly affects large parts of our society. For this reason, I think we should become better at critically examining the underlying reasons for our actions.

---

95   * Examples of educations in Denmark with the highest GPA entry requirements (2023); Uddannelses—og Forskningsstyrelsen (2021). *Hovedtal—Den Koordinerede Tilmelding (KOT)*

WHAT ABOUT THE NEXT GENERATION?

"I only feel good enough when I succeed in almost all areas of my life." In 2021, Danish young people aged 16-24 were asked how they thought about themselves. 56% agreed with the above statement.

Our opportunities seem to carry a weight, and sometimes we might forget that our youth bear the same burden. The difference is that they carry this weight without the same conditions or life experience as the rest of society. As a result, the downside of our choices and opportunities is particularly evident among our young people.

In the 2021 report by Danish Mental Health Fund, 41% of young people aged 16-24 stated that their self-esteem is tied to obtaining the right education and the right job. They compare themselves with the rest of society, where external factors seem to be the focal point of their happiness. Additionally, 31% of young people feel that their social circle appears to have a better life on social media, and 71% believe that as long as they "pull themselves together", they can achieve anything they want.[96]

---

96   Danish Mental Health Fund. Psykiatrifonden (2021). Translated from Danish to English: Original text: *"Jeg skal have succes på næsten alle områder af livet for at føle mig god nok."*

Many of the issues described in this book are also evident among the youth, but they often experience a greater impact. And understandably so, as they have grown up amidst an overabundance of options that shape them from an early age. We should therefore learn to question our role in order to best navigate a modern world, not just for ourselves but also for future generations, if we wish to address these issues effectively.

We know that dealing with too many options can lead to mental discomfort and contribute to psychological illnesses such as anxiety and depression. This phenomenon is observed in consumer behavior, where an abundance of choices leads to doubt and discomfort, and it is also discussed in philosophy. The existentialist philosopher Søren Kierkegaard explained that our anxiety can be seen as a counter-reaction to our freedom and the idea of having to take responsibility for oneself, a concept he described with the words: "Anxiety is the dizziness of freedom."[97]

As the world evolves, it appears that future generations will face even more choices. Recognizing this as a significant societal issue that clearly affects both our youth and the next generation is vital. A good starting point is to understand how we are influenced by our options and how we make our own decisions. Therefore, it is crucial to consider existentialist philosophy in practice.

---

97   Kierkegaard, S. (2018). *Begrebet angest.*

PART 6: EXISTENTIALIST PHILOSOPHY IN PRACTICE

"Life is not a problem to be solved,
but a reality to be experienced."
–Søren Kierkegaard

HOW TO USE EXISTENTIALIST PHILOSOPHY

How does existentialist thought relate to the way you perceive the world? And how do you apply this philosophy in practice?

In the second part of this book, you will be reading about how existentialist philosophy has been influenced by various philosophers. Each presents their unique perspective on what it means to live an existential life. But, how you utilize their thoughts also depends on your own interpretation.

They do not serve as definitive tools or a self-help guide that guarantees a happy life. Instead, they offer perspectives for your existence and the way you choose to shape it through your actions. How you apply these perspectives is as unique and subjective as the philosophers who shaped them. There is not one specific existential approach to life, but many. However, there are common threads in how this philosophy can be practiced.

Living a life inspired by existentialists, you are aware of your freedom and understand it must be seized through your actions. You seek creativity and you are brave enough to challenge what others think in order to prioritize what you believe. You dare to critically examine all preconceptions of life that could limit you and lead you to form an identity based on others' opinions. Similarly, you avoid pigeonholing others, remaining curious about them, just as you are about yourself. You focus on your internal values and create space to renew yourself and your understanding of which options bring value to you. You take responsibility for yourself, which is expressed through your actions.

You can contemplate these interpretations of an existential life as you explore how to apply them on your own. Together, they form a set of perspectives that can be used in the way you handle your options and the choices that follow. When we talk about existentialist philosophy, it is precisely these perspectives that should be lived out in practice.[98]

Philosophy and the abundance of choices

In this book, I have focused on the impact our choices can have on both our mental well-being and our self-perception. As the number of our choices increases, an alarming picture emerges where we find it increasingly difficult to handle the decisions that come with these options. This is also reflected in the rise of mental illness and discomfort among adults and young people in Denmark and much of the Western world. So, what do we do with our choices?

The studies presented in consumer behavior and modern psychology paint a rather unattractive picture. Questions like how to survive do not seem to dominate our decisions in the Western world. Instead, we appear to live in a world of prosperity and opportunities, where the primary reason for our actions is our desire for self-realization.

Despite our freedom, we experience a growing imbalance. Our modern society seems to have succeeded, in the sense that we have an abundance of options. But, at the same time, this success is also the cause of other problems, creating a paradox where our opportunities lead to mental disorders and fill us with a constant sense that we are missing out on something.

We are burdened by choices that weigh heavily on our mental well-being. A mental weight that leads us to take shortcuts and lim-

---

98   Gosetti-Ferencei, J. (2021). *On Being and Becoming: An Existentialist Approach to Life An Existentialist Approach to Life.*

it ourselves, while we try to compare ourselves with everyone else. This weight shifts our focus away from ourselves, while it is only ourselves who can create the value of our actions.

Mental traps

Based on the studies mentioned in the book, we can try to avoid a number of mental traps that seem to lead to psychological problems. If you want to apply existentialist philosophy in practice, it should be aimed at avoiding these traps.

Why? Because falling into these mental traps complicates your decision-making process. That means you make it harder for yourself to make the decisions that, according to existentialist thought, are crucial to living a good life. The mental traps—and how to avoid them—are outlined below. Each will be elaborated in the upcoming sections.

Mental traps

Avoid focusing on others: You can refrain from comparing yourself to others and make choices that create value for others instead of yourself.

Avoid perfectionism: You can stop yourself from over-analyzing your options and instead make choices that are just "good enough".

Avoid mental shortcuts: You can avoid letting your brain's mental shortcuts limit your choices by understanding how your brain values your options.

Avoid believing that more is better: You can avoid thinking that you need to consider more options and associate more choices with more value just because you have the opportunity.

> **Avoid the thought of missing out:** You can stop yourself from thinking about everything you believe you are missing out on and instead focus on seeing the value of what you already have.

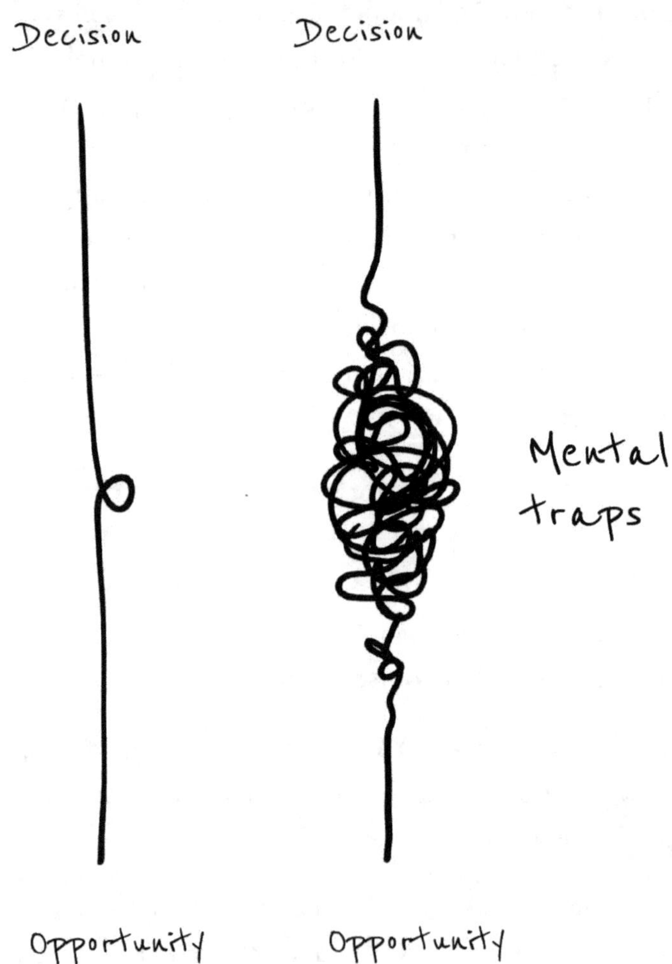

EXISTENTIALIST PERSPECTIVES

The purpose of exploring how to use existentialist philosophy in practice is to avoid the mental traps we set for ourselves. With the relevant theoretical knowledge about these traps, combined with existentialist philosophy, we can create the best conditions for focusing on ourselves.

In doing so, we can make it possible to create our own meaning from our actions.

This book presents seven selected perspectives from existentialist philosophy. Each perspective and its unique understanding of how we handle our options has its own section. But first, you can get an overview below and read what each perspective focuses on, which will be elaborated on in their respective sections later in the book.

The seven existentialist perspectives

1. The absurdity of life

The concept that life can appear absurd is a recurring theme in philosophy. Using this as a perspective on your actions can help you realize how the absurdity of life can actually be beneficial. The section focuses on how you relate to your life and choices when everything seems absurd and meaningless—and why it matters that you do.

2. Anxiety

Anxiety is also a prominent theme in existentialist philosophy, and it is also one of the significant consequences of our choices. This section presents how philosophy can help you process the anxiety that comes with your freedom and the multitude of options you encounter.

3. Authenticity

Being authentic is crucial to living an existentialist life, which should be reflected in your actions. But it can be difficult to include yourself in all the choices you make—because you make so many of them. The section explains how philosophy can offer a vital perspective on your actions, aiding in the pursuit of authenticity.

4. Dependence on others

As seen in studies from psychology and consumer behavior, the many options we have can lead you to seek acceptance from other people. They can give you the idea that you need other people's acceptance and material goods to be happy. But according to existentialist philosophy, you are in danger of becoming dependent on things that extend beyond yourself. And in the end, it is you who defines what makes you happy. Philosophy can remind you of this, so you become less dependent on other people when making decisions.

5. Focus on the present

It becomes both harder and more important to focus on the present. But as a result of your many options, and a modern world where it is possible to communicate at all hours, you risk losing this focus. However, it is in the present that you find the value of your choices according to existentialist philosophy. The section, therefore, focuses on how you can maintain focus on the present.

6. Daring to fail

More options arise, while more people seem to have a desire not to make mistakes. When these two things are combined, it becomes a dangerous cocktail where you can feel that you have to make more choices, but also always avoid stepping off the path. These two things do not work well together. This book presents how you can benefit from learning that it is an art to dare to fail.

7. Death

For many of us, death is not a subject that is discussed daily. However, philosophy believes that you can benefit from learning to relate to death, as it can put an important perspective on your actions. And as you will read in the section, you can even learn to use death to focus on what matters.

After the above perspectives have been elaborated, the discussion will go on by underlining the importance of recognizing your choices as a privilege, and an opportunity to utilize.

1. Perspective: The absurdity of life and the myth of Sisyphus

In 1942, Albert Camus published the book "The Myth of Sisyphus". In his book, he tells the story of King Sisyphus from Greek mythology, who tricked and opposed the gods. As punishment, he was condemned to push a stone up a mountain, but every time the stone reached the top, it rolled back down, and he had to push it up again. And he had to do this over and over for eternity. In the story of Sisyphus, Camus describes the absurdity of life, our actions have no meaning, but we perform them anyway. Like Sisyphus, who was forever doomed to push the stone up the mountain only to watch it roll down again.

Camus believes that, like Sisyphus, we are doomed to perform meaningless actions over and over. Life, therefore, seems absurd and without any greater meaning. However, Camus explains that as soon as Sisyphus acknowledged the absurdity of his life, he made it possible to free himself. Knowing that he had to push the stone up the mountain for the rest of his days made him aware that his entire life was absurd. At that moment, he also chose to accept his situation, which helps illustrate how we as humans can find beauty in everything. Even when it all seems absurd.

Like Sisyphus, you have the choice to recognize and accept the absurd rather than suppress it; and herein lies the difference, according to Camus. You can choose to see life as meaningless and not accept that life is absurd, thereby condemning your life. But you can also choose to see life as meaningful, despite it appearing absurd and meaningless. Ultimately, it is up to you to assess the meaning of your actions and your life. As Camus describes it:

> "If this myth is tragic, that is because its hero is
> conscious. Where would his torture be, indeed, if at
> every step the hope of succeeding upheld him?"[99]

In other words: what if Sisyphus views his actions as successful? In this case, they are not meaningless, despite seeming so to others. As long as Sisyphus refuses to focus on how his situation may appear, choosing instead to focus on how he himself defines it, his actions gain significance. However, this requires him to become aware of his actions, which he does when he realizes that he has to push the stone up the mountain forever. Camus explains this in his work with the words:

---

99   Translated to English from the Danish version of the book. Camus, A.(1942). *Sisyfos-Myten*, s. 115

"The lucidity that was to constitute his torture at the
same time crowns his victory. There is no fate that
cannot be surmounted by scorn.[100]

The absurdity of life arises when a person seeks to understand
the world and the meaning of life but refuses to accept that the
world cannot provide the answer. Camus believes that we stand
alone in an absurd world, just like Sisyphus. We must ourselves
choose whether to see our actions as meaningless or significant. We
can also choose to embrace our absurd fate, where life is sometimes
seen as a struggle, but nonetheless is our own. As Camus explains:

"Sisyphus is, as you can see, the absurd hero. He
is that in his passions and his torment. It was his
contempt for the gods, his hatred of death, and his
passion for life that brought upon him the dreadful
punishment of having to exert all his strength toward
achieving nothing. That is the price that must be paid
for the pleasures of this world."[101]

Let go of control

It was only when Sisyphus let go and stopped trying to control
his situation that he found meaning in his actions. As studies in
consumer behavior and psychology have shown us, we, as humans,
try to control our options. This is evident in our need to analyze
and make the best decision, as well as our attempt to execute all
our actions to perfection. However, as already explained, neither
excessive analysis of our options nor a life marked by perfectionism leads to greater joy in life. On the contrary, it can have the

---

100   Translated to English from the Danish version of the book. Camus, A.(1942).
Sisyfos-Myten, p. 115

101   Translated to English from the Danish version of the book. Camus, A.(1942).
Sisyfos-Myten, p. 114

opposite effect. There appears to be a parallel between the theory of consumer behavior and the philosophers, both of which help us understand that we need to learn to let go of our need for control.

Jean-Paul Sartre believes that if we do not accept that life is absurd, we will try to control everything around us. And according to him, this is not very good. He describes it as trying to be God by creating full control over our own destiny. This stems from the existentialist thought that as humans we are born completely free, and therefore the meaning of our lives is also created through the choices we make—or do not make. As Sartre explains:

> " I can always choose, but I ought to know that if
> I do not choose, I am still choosing.[102]

Sartre posits that attempting to create meaning from our surroundings is akin to playing God, as it involves transforming something absurd and inherently meaningless into something with greater significance. This is an impossible endeavor, leading us on a hopeless quest for a greater meaning that does not exist, due to our refusal to accept life's absurdity.

Reflect on the last significant project you worked on. You might have worked towards a specific outcome, hoping for a desired response: perhaps a "well done" from your boss, a top grade in your final project, or a sense of happiness from surprising your partner.

Here, the existentialist mindset can be applied to focus on why you perform your actions. If you accept that life is absurd, you must also accept that only you can create meaning for your actions. Therefore, when you submit your project, you should not make your joy dependent on the response you hope to receive. That is out of your control. What is not out of your control, however, is the meaning you attach to your actions. If you do not receive a pat

---

102   JP Sartre, J. (2015). *Existentialism and Human Emotions.*

on the back and a "well done" from your boss, the top grade you wanted for your assignment, or if your partner seems indifferent to your surprise, you must still hold on to the joy of making an effort that is still yours because you attributed value to it.

The pat on the back, the top grade, or your partner's happiness could momentarily seem crucial for your happiness, but according to the philosophy, this would make your happiness dependent on their assessment of something that, in reality, is absurd. After all, it is just work, a project, or a surprise. There can be freedom in telling yourself that your actions always mean more to you than to others. You cannot control how others react to what you do. Accepting life's absurdity is thus a prerequisite for letting go of control. According to philosophy, it is futile to try to control a life that is already absurd. Instead, the task is to focus on how you can enjoy it.

2. Perspective: Life and anxiety

Anxiety is a recurring theme in existentialist philosophy, where it is linked to the number of our options. Anxiety manifests when we ask ourselves if we are fully living our lives and if we are making the right decisions. It emerges when we doubt whether we are good enough or if others have a better life than us.

According to consumer behavior studies, the multitude of our options puts pressure on us, as we may focus on what we might lose rather than what we could gain. Additionally, our brains can become overloaded when presented with an increasing number of options. As a countermeasure, the brain attempts to take mental shortcuts, where various cognitive biases can limit us in decision-making. We can even feel uncomfortably when choosing among too many options, partly because we feel a loss of control.

Here, anxiety is a reaction to our environment, as psychiatrist Ronald Laing (2010) described it.[103] It is our natural reaction to

---

103   Laing, R. D. (2010). *The Divided Self—An Existential Study in Sanity and Madness.*

everything around us that feels dangerous. As our environment presents more options, our anxiety increases. This is evident in the consequences of our options, including that about 700,000 Danish adults suffer from psychological disorders, with anxiety being one of the most common. Among Danish youth, we also see an increase in anxiety when they feel they need to do everything perfectly. But not only that, they simultaneously feel the need to achieve more and more. They must not miss out on their opportunities, which contributes to a rise in psychological illnesses, particularly anxiety.

A response to freedom

As Søren Kierkegaard describes, anxiety is a response to our freedom. Anxiety arises when we feel threatened, and our environment seems dangerous. So, what makes us associate our options with something dangerous? And how can we use existentialist philosophy to counter this?

Studies on consumer behavior show that we cannot deal with too many options, while psychological studies emphasize that we cannot help but compare ourselves to others. In other words, we cannot avoid comparing ourselves to others, and it seems impossible to avoid our options. As Søren Kierkegaard explains, life is associated with anxiety because we are free and have the option to choose. Trying to avoid anxiety will only make it worse, as we will suppress it through our actions. Therefore, it is not something we can or should avoid, as this only exacerbates the problem. As he writes:

> "Anxiety is the reality of freedom as
> the possibility of possibility."[104]

The options you face do not just have a single possible consequence but rather an infinite number. The thought of the many

---

104   Translated to English from the Danish version of the book. Kierkegaard, S. (2018). *Begrebet angest.*

possible consequences of your choices—or lack thereof—creates anxiety because you do not know the outcome of your actions. Therefore, there is no freedom without anxiety. Something similar was described in consumer behavior as opportunity costs, which explains how we value our choices based on the alternatives we have to give up. The lost value from our alternatives can be seen as the consequence of our choices, which causes us anxiety because we know what we might miss out on.

Like Sisyphus, we can be struck by a feeling of indifference in our actions, which can even make freedom feel dangerous. The very definition of anxiety is that it acts as a natural reaction to something that feels dangerous.[105]

Understanding the freedom and significance of its opportunities on our thoughts is therefore crucial for our ability to see our options as something positive. According to Kierkegaard, it is our relationship with freedom that causes anxiety because we feel that we have to choose. If we try to suppress the need to choose and ignore the many opportunities that our freedom brings, it will only create a greater sense of anxiety. Instead, according to Kierkegaard, we should recognize that our anxiety requires us to consider our freedom and its opportunities by taking action. Only then do we take something unreal (like our freedom) and make it real. Common to his ideas and the entire existentialist movement is that freedom must be seized, and we do so through the choices we make.

In relation to our options, anxiety is expressed when we face a large number of decisions that we feel we have to consider. Here we can come to believe that we must realize all our opportunities. We end up filling our daily lives with a large number of choices that drain our mental energy.

---

105   *https://psykiatrifonden.dk/diagnoser/angst*

When our options seem dangerous—and anxiety is expressed—it can be seen as a counter-reaction to not focusing on our own choices, but on others' instead. We feel that we have to achieve something because others say so, which is why we try to make all the right decisions and execute them to perfection.

But perfection is not linked to joy. It has even been documented that as humans, we feel happier when we focus on ourselves and dare to be satisfied with things that are good enough. We can therefore advantageously choose the first thing that seems satisfactory instead of chasing the understanding of perfection. Something Herbert Simon (1947) also described with the term 'satisficing' earlier in the book. The alternative is that we will focus on everyone else but ourselves, whereby what we do will lose its meaning.

Before Sisyphus realized that his actions were absurd, his punishment was the worst possible thing he could be subjected to. It was only when he began to recognize the absurdity of his actions that he made it possible to find value in his life. If you think that you have to do everything to perfection, take comfort in the fact that research shows you will be happier when you chase what seems good enough—instead of chasing what seems perfect.

Our expectations and anxiety

According to author and philosopher Allain de Botton (2005), our anxiety is a result of our reality not living up to our expectations.[106] It can be easy to fall into the trap of thinking there is a universal definition of happiness and, for instance, telling oneself that one must have a successful job, a good relationship, and a big house to be happy. Fortunately, reality is different. But recognizing this requires you to dare to think about what you associate with being happy. It may be that your ideas of what makes you happy are not the same as what actually makes you happy.

---

106   Botton, A. D. (2005). *Status Anxiety.*

Anxiety seems to accompany our freedom when we realize that we can do almost anything. In our quest for meaning, we try to analyze our way to our best choices. This leads us to seek everything that can be good for us. But as we give ourselves more, we also expect more. We can therefore find ourselves trapped in the understanding that we must have as much good as possible, and that all bad must be removed from our lives.

Here, Nietzsche explains that humans experience life in contradictions. Nietzsche argues that good only exists because bad also exists. If we only surround ourselves with what feels good and even make it our mission in life to avoid everything bad, the good also loses its meaning. As a result, the value of our choices also diminishes.

We only start to appreciate the little things in life when we feel a need for them. Think back to the last time you were really thirsty and finally quenched your thirst. The water tasted amazing then. But only because you were thirsty. If you had drunk a large glass of water beforehand, the feeling probably would not have been the same. The feeling of discomfort, and the lack of something, thus brings a sense of value to the choices you make. Nietzsche believes that we reduce the value of our choices in life if we try to remove everything that feels unpleasant. To this, he poses the question:

> "What if pleasure and displeasure were so tied
> together that whoever wanted to have as much as
> possible of one must also have as much as possible of
> the other (...)"[107]

You might be trying to avoid everything bad in your life. However, your pursuit of perfection and a life without flaws has its consequences, as explained by existentialist philosophy. The quest

---

107   Nietzsche, F. W. (1974). *The Gay Science: With a Prelude in Rhymes and an Appendix of Songs.*

for a perfect life without discomforts makes your life fragile. Why? Because you focus on what you can lose, not on all that you can possibly gain. This causes you to try to hold onto everything you have by controlling your choices. And as the number of your options increases, so does your need for control. A dangerous cycle of more options and more control begins. But neither makes you happier.

A life without discomfort, according to Nietzsche, leads to a limited life. As Nietzsche puts it, you have to choose whether you want a life where you accept its bad sides, then to enjoy its good sides. You cannot both live a life free from pain and discomfort and expect to find meaning and joy in your actions. As he writes:

> "You have the choice: either as little displeasure
> as possible, painlessness in brief... or as much
> displeasure as possible as the price for the growth of
> an abundance of subtle pleasures and joys that have
> rarely been relished yet? If you decide for the former
> and desire to diminish and lower the level of human
> pain, you also have to diminish and lower the level of
> their capacity for joy."[108]

The downside of our striving for a life without confronting life's unpleasant aspects, as Nietzsche explains, also leads to a lack of joy. We cannot have the sweet without the bitter.

Like Sisyphus, you can make your life a punishment if you try to avoid your discomfort. But you can also see it as a gift if you accept the unpleasantness. Only then—in the midst of the absurdity of your life—can you find meaning in life through your actions.

---

108   "Ffom the book Nietzsche, F. W. (1974). *The Gay Science: With a Prelude in Rhymes and an Appendix of Songs.*

3. Perspective: An authentic life

Existentialist philosophy tells us that it is not the objective value of our choices that matters to us. Instead, it is the subjective value that we ourselves assign to our choices that gives value.

As described in earlier sections of the book, you may be led to believe that you should make as many choices as possible because your opportunities allow it. However, it would be more beneficial to focus on what matters to you and prioritize that instead. Yet, this requires you to challenge the notion that more is better. The same applies to the idea that there is a definitive right answer to everything that can guarantee a good life. Both are traps that humans can fall into, according to existentialist philosophy, which also explains that the only truth is your own. It is only through yourself that you can decide what gives value and meaning to your life.

Responsibility for your own freedom

According to existentialist philosophy, you live an authentic life by taking responsibility for your own freedom, and the way you choose to express it through your actions. Therefore, you should not limit yourself to believing that you have to live in a certain way. At the same time, you should also relate to other people's freedom without reducing them to objects, but instead, engage with the many opportunities they face—just like yourself.

Nietzsche believes that we must take responsibility for our choices and the consequences that follow, before we can live an authentic life. He proposed an experiment to explore which areas of life one unconsciously wishes to change in order to live authentically. As part of the experiment, you ask yourself:

> What things would you change in your life if you
> knew you had to relive them forever?[109]

---

109   Nietzsche, F. W. (1974). *The Gay Science: With a Prelude in Rhymes and an Appendix of Songs.*

What would you answer? Is there anything you would immediately do differently? What things—and why? You can also think about what you wish you had done instead. When we relate Nietzsche's thought experiment about our authenticity to our opportunities, you can ask yourself the same questions: What choices would you have avoided if you could? Do you continue to make the same choices even though you regret them? And if so, what stops you from refraining from making them?

It might be that you feel unhappy because of the choices you have made earlier in life. Perhaps you are not content with your career path or the study you chose to pursue? You have the opportunity to do something about it, but perhaps you choose not to. It could be that you feel you have invested too much time and resources in getting to where you are today. In that case, you are limiting your understanding of your options by falling into various mental shortcuts. You overestimate the value of what you have, while failing to see your past as a sunk cost. Here, it is relevant to quote Sartre's play "The Flies" (1943), where he poses the question:

"Why distort a past that can no longer
stand up for itself?"[110]

Or in other words: why cling to the belief that your past was wrong if it was right at the time? Instead, relate to the present by telling yourself that you are free to choose. Do not let your past create unnecessary noise that distracts your focus from the present. Returning to Nietzsche's experiment, we might appropriately ask ourselves whether we are burying our own identity by performing actions we do not want to repeat. If so, we are making inauthentic decisions.

Here, existentialist philosophy explains that you can let your freedom be constrained by what you think you should do. But in

---

110   Jean-Paul Sartre's play "The Flies" (1943)

reality, there is nothing you must do. There are only things you can do. And it takes root in your own wishes, as they are the only actions where you remain authentic.

We can easily cling to a false value of our past decisions, believing they have greater worth than they do. Therefore, we might stick to a career path, a bad relationship, or unhealthy social relations, telling ourselves we cannot do anything about it. But if you do not want to relive those things—forever—then they are not authentic for you, Nietzsche believes.

A conflict between your inner and outer self

It may seem abstract to consider that all your choices should be authentic. But it can also be a healthy perspective to form on your life choices. It can lead you to assess who you allow to influence your choices when it should really only be yourself.

Humanistic psychologist Carl Rogers (1995) explains that we have a biological drive to move towards our true self. This happens when we make authentic decisions. According to Rogers, a person can only function optimally when connected with their values and emotions, thus their inner self. This creates stability in the actions we take. Why? Because we do not change the way we are, even when we change our surroundings and are with new people. Or as Rogers states, we do not deviate based on our surroundings, therefore we remain authentic in the choices we make.[111]

Studies have also shown that we achieve greater well-being and mental happiness when we are authentic. Among other benefits, we become more independent, have more positive thoughts about ourselves and others, and it reduces both stress and anxiety.[112]

---

111   Rogers, C. (1995). *On Becoming a Person: A Therapist's View of Psychotherapy.*

112   Wood, A. M., Linley, P. A., Maltby, J., Baliousis M. & Joseph, S. (2008). *The Authentic Personality: A Theoretical and Empirical Conceptualization and the Development of the Authenticity Scale.*

Consider two people who choose to remain married even though they are unhappy. They might tell themselves that staying together seems the most logical choice. This way, they still fit into the concept of the nuclear family and the ideal life, where the mother and father are married. However, if they no longer love each other, staying together would only be inauthentic, according to existentialist philosophy.

Why? Because they remove responsibility from themselves and avoid addressing their freedom. It is fear that keeps them together, not their own desires. A fear of not being able to place themselves in the common understanding of a man and woman in a marriage. Thus, they avoid their freedom in the same way as the waiter in Sartre's story, who assumed the role of a waiter but, in the process, also repressed his own identity. He sacrificed his authentic self to buy into a role created by others. Similarly, the married couple would rather live unhappily together than give up their role as a married couple. This illustrates the conflict we can all experience between our inner and outer selves—how we want to be versus how we want others to see us.

We can forget to be authentic by placing ourselves in a specific role and risk sacrificing our authenticity to fit in. Existentialist philosophy believes the reason for our inauthentic actions arises from a conflict between the inner and outer self. This is expressed when you try to stage yourself as something other than what you feel. In the presence of others, you might try to appear in a specific way. But if your outer self does not reflect your inner self, you will act inauthentically.

When we allow our outer self to dictate our inner self, we place the responsibility for our freedom in the hands of others rather than ourselves, which contradicts the idea of an authentic life. If your actions are performed to please your outer self, it will create a conflict, as you try to appear in a specific way that conflicts with your inner being, at the expense of your values. This can lead to psychological disorders like anxiety, explains Rogers. This could be seen in the example of the unhappy married couple staying together to maintain an external image at the cost of their inner values. It could also be the perfectionist employee or student who does everything not to make mistakes. In this case, existentialist thought explains that the person is trying to maintain an outer self that does not make mistakes. However, if this contradicts their inner self, where making mistakes is part of living, it creates a conflict. This can lead to anxiety and other psychological illnesses.

An ambiguous life

In the classic existentialist book "The Ethics of Ambiguity" from 1947, the philosopher Simone de Beauvoir describes how humans live an ambiguous life.[113] We do not think the same about ourselves all the time, but instead, we change our understanding of who we are. Yet, we try to define ourselves as something definitive in an attempt to make sense of the person we believe we are. This contradicts existentialism, which explains that we should not deny our ambiguous nature and try to ascribe ourselves a fixed identity.

Instead, we should recognize that we are different based on the actions we take. Consider the person who enjoys their job but also plays music in a band in their free time. Should the person choose between an identity as an office worker or a musician? No, not necessarily, according to Beauvoir, who explains that your identity has multiple sides. Therefore, you should not limit it to one thing because you think you must behave in one specific way. She explains that you behave differently based on what you do—and there is nothing wrong with that. Having multiple identities is not the same as suppressing your own identity. On the contrary, it just shows that you dare to unfold your full identity and its many different sides.

By not having a fixed identity, we choose to free ourselves by saying that we do not need to confine and limit our actions.

---

113   Beauvoir, S. (1997). *En tvetydighedens moral.*

Herein lies one of the most important messages from existentialist thought: life is undoubtedly complicated. But instead of denying its complexity, we should ask ourselves how we can face this complexity. For the same reason, existentialist philosophy also denies moral doctrines that can cause people to forget their own identity and blindly follow others' unethical actions. Beauvoir compares it to the many people who blindly followed the Nazi regime without questioning what they stood for.

According to existential philosophy, your identity is ambiguous and contains several different sides, all of which should be allowed to influence your choices. Do you want to be an office-working musician who also likes to play amateur theater on weekends? Fine. As long as you remain authentic and do the things you want, you can do what you like. The concept of identity and the idea that you should do some things in extension of that identity will only serve to limit your freedom—and therefore also the way you relate to your opportunities. The problem should not be whether you can do the things you want, but your ability to figure out what you want to do.

You are "condemned to be free," as Sartre describes it. Yes, you are free, but it also requires you to figure out what you should do to acknowledge your freedom. According to existentialist philosophy, you must remain true to your inner self to live an authentic life. You should not be disturbed by your outer self or wait to find meaning in life through your surroundings, even though you should be able to relate to them. In the end, an authentic and meaningful life can only be created if it is based on your inner self.

4. Perspective: Dependent on others

Studies in psychology and consumer behavior have shown that we place great value on others' assessments of us as individuals. We can become dependent on these evaluations, but it is not necessarily good to rely on others, especially if one aims to live an authentic life as proposed by existentialist philosophy.

Part of comparing ourselves to others can lead us to let others determine if we should be happy. Existentialist philosophy tells us to shift focus away from others, as only we can define our own happiness.

When you compare yourself to others, it might be because you are trying to confirm the value of your choices. For instance, you might decide to buy a new pair of shoes. Before purchasing, you check who else has bought the same shoes. Perhaps you scrolled through Instagram and saw someone with a great taste wearing them. You compare yourself to that person, and their choice to buy the same shoes enhances the value of your decision to buy them too. After purchasing them, you might seek to reconfirm their worth.

In this process, existentialist philosophy emphasizes that you might be making more inauthentic decisions than you realize. Firstly, you might convince yourself that you need new shoes because you compare yourself to others, thereby creating a need that does not genuinely exist (unless your old shoes are broken). The need stems from another person, so you are shifting focus away from your inner self and its needs. Instead, you let your external self take over, influencing your decision.

But this does not just apply to buying shoes. Another example could be starting a new job and seeking validation for your decision by telling everyone how great your new workplace is. You might find yourself constantly saying how wonderful your colleagues are and how much better the tasks are than at your previous job. It is the same process, seeking validation from others because you cannot stop comparing yourself to them. Other examples include starting a study program and wanting to confirm you have made the right choice, or ensuring you have selected the right Netflix series by reading all the reviews you can find. "Did the series get five stars?"

Focus on yourself

We strive to be as certain as possible about the choices we make, leading us to compare ourselves to others. However, existentialist philosophy suggests that the answer to whether we have made the right decision cannot be found in others. In a scene from one of his plays, Jean-Paul Sartre highlights the danger of such comparisons, using the stark phrase: "Hell is other people". Sartre and existentialist philosophy urge us to explore the reasons behind our choices. It is easier to seek answers from others, but this only offers a temporary fix—like a band-aid—as the ultimate answer must come from within ourselves.

Sartre described humans as "condemned to be free", elaborating as follows:

> "Condemned, because he did not create himself, in other respect is free; because, once thrown into the world, he is responsible for everything he does."[114]

As he explains, responsibility comes with your freedom. A freedom that can be difficult to handle, but from which there is no escape. Ultimately, it can only be shaped and managed by yourself. According to existentialist philosophy, becoming independent of others involves focusing on oneself. However, in an increasingly complex world, this can seem challenging. Here, we can turn to Søren Kierkegaard, who suggests that we do not need to compare ourselves with others in an attempt to stand out. We are all special, not necessarily because of our ability to be different from others, but because we are unique in ourselves. After all, there is no one else quite like you. If you try to stand out, you may end up chasing a false version of yourself.

Kierkegaard believes that freedom—and finding oneself—is not about creating an identity to show others how special we are.

---

114   Sartre, J. (1993). *Being and Nothingness.*

On the contrary, it is the opposite of being free if you chase something that you are not, in reality. Instead, you should strive to be yourself, which requires standing alone with your actions without expecting a specific response from others. As Kierkegaard explains in his work "Kjerlighedens Gjerninger" from 1847 (Works of Love):[115]

> "The highest thing one person can do for another is
> to make him free, help him to stand alone."[116]

According to Kierkegaard, the best thing you can do for other people, and for yourself as well, is to teach the other person how to stand alone.

Choosing for yourself

Research has shown that we often derive more joy from our actions when they are guided by intuition and creativity. The existentialist philosophy also encourages you to break free from norms and cultivate your creative side. As Nietzsche explains, our creativity can serve as a useful tool in discovering who we are, after which we can act as artists in our own lives, creating and forging our own meaning.

But before we can create meaning, we need to liberate ourselves from dependency on others. This starts with our understanding that there is a definitive right answer. If you feel that happiness is just around the corner, existentialist philosophy would suggest you are deceiving yourself. You will not find an objective answer to your happiness among other people. Chasing a definitive answer only leads to dependence on others because you might come to believe that they know something you do not. They might be

---

115   In Danish "Kjerlighedens Gjerninger" (1847)

116   Translated to English. Original Danish text: "det Høieste, det ene Menneske kan gjøre for det andet, er at gjøre ham fri, hjælpe ham til at staae ene" in the book Kierkegaard, S. (2013). *Kjerlighedens Gjerninger.*

pursuing different things, which creates an anxiety that they have found a direction in life of greater value than your own. As Albert Camus writes in his book "The Plague" from 1947:

> "You can't understand. You're using the language
> of reason, not of the heart; you live in a world of...
> of abstractions."[117]

Camus is essentially saying: do not try to understand all your options, or what seems to make sense to others. Instead, focus on yourself. Do not let your options become notions of what you think you lack, but rather follow what you yourself desire. We try to do everything we can not to miss out on anything. But paradoxically, in our attempt to have it all, we also risk missing out on more. As Camus explains:

> "The habit of despair is worse than despair itself."[118]

It can be easy to believe that you are missing out on something, which seeds doubt about your actions, ultimately leading to anxiety. An anxiety created by the fear that you are not realizing the full potential of your freedom. But a focus on not wanting to miss out leads you to concentrate on your past and future, while forgetting your present. When this happens, you trap yourself in despair over your own actions. Doubt that can become a habit, as Camus explains. If that happens, you will focus more on what you think you are missing out on, while in reality, you are missing everything that is happening in front of you right now. Therefore, tell yourself that there is no right or wrong answer. It is better to just choose—and be satisfied with good enough—otherwise, you will miss everything around you in an attempt to find a right answer that does not exist.

---

117   Camus, A. (2012). *The Plague.*

118   Camus, A. (2012). *The Plague.*

Jean-Paul Sartre believes that the path to making your own choices lies in the ability to follow your own beliefs. In your own understanding of the world, you find the answer to which choices you should make, as ultimately only you can define what is right and wrong.

To illustrate his point, Sartre describes an anecdote involving one of his students who faced a difficult decision. He could either join the military and fight in World War II or stay back to take care of his sick mother. The student himself believed that participating in the war was the right decision. But he was also worried about his mother, who depended on him. If he went to war, he would not be able to help his mother and would most likely not see her again. But he had to make a choice.

On the one hand, he could join an important cause, where he would be a small part in a larger fight for freedom that would affect millions of people. Or he could stay with his mother and play a significant role for a single person. He felt a responsibility for both and did not know what to choose. Here, Sartre argued that there was no answer until the student himself made a decision. In the end, neither of his options was right or wrong. Therefore, there was no choice other than his own that would be authentic. The only right choice was the one he himself made.[119]

In perspective to our modern world, full of freedom and opportunities, Sartre explains that none of the options you decide to pursue will be right until you choose to follow them yourself. It is only you who can give value to the choice you make, as opposed to the many other options you reject. If you want to tell yourself that the decision you have made is the best, then it will also be the best. Conversely, if you wish to tell yourself that a different decision could have been better than the one you took, then that alternative decision will also appear better.

---

119   Sartre, J. (2007). *Existentialism is a Humanism.*

The danger of following in others' footsteps

There is a story from ancient Greece when Alexander the Great visited the city of Corinth to meet the philosopher Diogenes, who was particularly known for living a minimalist life, which was evident in his choice to live in a barrel.

When Alexander met Diogenes, he asked how he could help him. At that time, Alexander was one of the most powerful people in the world, making Diogenes extremely privileged and fortunate to have the opportunity to have a wish fulfilled by the emperor.[120] To Alexander's question, the philosopher replied, "Yes, if you could move a little. You're blocking the sun."

People were astonished at his response, and Alexander's men began to laugh. They wondered why Diogenes had not asked for wealth, status, or something of value? But Diogenes lived according to his principles and what was important to him. He did not value the same things as others, but rather simply to enjoy the moment in the sun. After receiving this unexpected answer, Alexander did not get angry, as one might have expected. Instead, he admired Diogenes' response. And as they left, Alexander said to his men, who were still laughing over the situation, "If I were not Alexander, I would wish to be Diogenes."[121]

The crowd and Alexander the Great's companions had expected Diogenes to ask for status and money, but those things held no value for him. It was the present moment and the time in the sun that held the greatest value.

In our modern society, we feel drawn to realize the goals that others tell us are right. It is the compelling effect of a comparison culture that can lead us to choose things that do not make us happy. Had Diogenes followed what others thought he should have asked for, he would have asked for money, power, and status. But even

---

120   Dillon, J. M. (2004). *Morality and custom in ancient Greece.*

121   Botton, A. D. (2005). *Status Anxiety.*

if he had gotten all that, what then? He could sit on a large farm, with a lot of money, but if it did not make him happy, what was the point? An existentialist approach would follow the same understanding: happiness is something subjective, not objective. The story of Diogenes tells us not to blindly believe that something has value just because others say it does.

The existentialist philosophy sees our need to compare ourselves—and follow in others' footsteps—as a threat to our authenticity. Sartre believes that we follow others' footsteps because it gives us some frameworks for life that can help us handle the responsibility that comes with our freedom. We have difficulty accepting that we have no obligations, but that we are actually completely free. Therefore, we set up our own obligations, because it limits the responsibility and anxiety that comes with our freedom. If we do not feel that something binds us, or tells us what to do, then there is no one but ourselves to hold accountable. At the same time, it also means that all our actions have consequences, as we cannot blame others for the choices we make. It is therefore not about handing over our responsibility to others, but rather about choosing what we want in life, as this is how we manage to create the person we want to be.

Get to know yourself

There is one person you cannot escape, and with whom you will spend the rest of your life: yourself.

So maybe you should get to know that person. If you know yourself completely, you will also know what you want to do, no matter what situation you are in.

The existentialist philosophy tells us that we find meaning in life by making decisions based on our own feelings and thoughts. That no decisions or options we choose are wrong, as long as we decide of our own will that we want to carry them out. As the philosophy explains to us, we find joy through ourselves, and we find joy through action. Therefore, we should not be afraid to get to know ourselves, and we should not be afraid to take action and remove what stops us from achieving it.

Acknowledge our similarities

Existentialist philosophy focuses on the individual and views the human tendency to compare oneself to others as detrimental to one's authenticity. However, the philosophy also believes that it can be advantageous to recognize our similarities; that we are more alike than we think.

You can feel it in a variety of situations, such as when your name is called incorrectly at a coffee bar. You are lost in your own thoughts, but then the mistake reminds you that the world is actually bigger than your thoughts alone.

According to the philosophy, finding meaning in life is not about separation oneself from others. Being authentic is not about seeking recognition from others, but rather about being curious about oneself. Therefore, it is important to also be curious about others. Kierkegaard describes it in his work "Kjerlighedens Gjerninger" (Works of Love):

> "You should love yourself in the same way you love
> your neighbor, when you love him as yourself"[122]

Here, Kierkegaard believes that the love for oneself arises at the same moment as you find love for others. Only when you can see yourself in others and love them, can you manage to love yourself. This implies that to be authentic towards yourself, you must first be authentic towards others around you as well as your environment. It is not about distancing oneself from others, but about remaining curious.

---

122   Translated to English. Original Danish text: "Du skal elske Dig selv saaledes, som Du elsker Næste" From the book, S. Kierkegaard (2013). *Kjerlighedens Gjerninger*

Research has shown that we cannot help but compare ourselves. However, if we choose to compare ourselves to others—based on the mindset that we are similar—we can avoid believing that others know something we do not. By doing this, you can evade the thought that other people's actions have greater value than your own.

Personally, I find it comforting to tell myself that no one cares as much about what I do as I do myself. It helps me to shift focus away from others and focus on what I do. Typically, what I choose to do always matters more to me than it does to others. And there is nothing wrong with that. Acknowledging this can be soothing because it can put one's thoughts into perspective. Here, you can ask yourself: are you making something out to be bigger than it really is? What if you chose not to do something, who else would care (besides yourself)? Are you trying to find meaning in what you do among others, while simultaneously forgetting to ask yourself why do you want to do it? According to existential philosophy, you can direct focus on yourself and thereby remove a dependency on others.

5. Perspective: Lack of focus on the present

In a 2010 article from Harvard, psychologists Matthew Killingsworth and Daniel Gilbert explain that on average, we spend 46.9% of our waking hours thinking about something other than what we are currently doing. This means that nearly half of our waking hours are spent focusing on things not immediately relevant to our current actions. But how does this affect our mental well-being? The two psychologists briefly explain:

> "A human mind is a wandering mind, and a
> wandering mind is an unhappy mind."[123]

---

123   Bradt, S. (2010). *Wandering mind not a happy mind.*

According to Killingsworth and Gilbert, our wandering minds pose a threat to our well-being. In their study, they surveyed 2,250 participants, randomly asking them throughout the day how happy they were, what they were doing, and whether they were thinking about the activity they were engaged in. They also inquired how their thoughts about the activity affected their feelings. Based on the data collected, the researchers found a correlation between the frequency of mind-wandering and happiness levels. Their study revealed that it is more than twice as important to focus on what you are doing, rather than what you are actually doing. Therefore, losing focus on the present moment and what you are currently doing is more likely to lead to feelings of unhappiness. Your ability to stay present is therefore a good indicator of your happiness.

Unlike other animals, humans spend a considerable amount of time thinking about things that are not happening at the moment. Our thoughts drift to past events, future occurrences, or things we imagine might happen, even though they often do not. There are countless examples, and our imagination is limitless, but most of us can probably relate to thinking about something other than the present moment.[124]

The need for religion and philosophy can largely be traced back to the human desire to remain in the present moment. This is evident in practices like meditation, prayer in religious contexts, and several themes addressed in philosophy. They all share the common goal of encouraging focus on the present. Existentialist philosophy also places significant importance on the present. According to this philosophical view, you cannot truly experience the world until you connect with it, which happens by being in the present moment. It is only in the present that you can act and realize your freedom. Albert Camus, in his 1942 novel "The Stranger," encapsulates this idea, writing:

---

124   Bradt, S. (2010). *Wandering mind not a happy mind*

"If something is going to happen to me,
I want to be there"[125]

What causes our thoughts to drift away, leading us to ponder on the past, future, and fantasies? More importantly, how does this impact our handling of opportunities?

The importance of the present

It is in the present moment that we connect with our senses, absorbing everything they offer us. In short, the present has a greater value that we sometimes forget to acknowledge.

But does this mean we should forget our past? Should we suppress our imagination and thoughts about the future to focus solely on the present? It may seem that existentialist philosophy advocates for an exclusive focus on the present. However, it is not about disregarding the past or future entirely. Rather, the philosophy suggests prioritizing the present over the past and future. It is in the present that you act. The philosophy centers on what you can change and, therefore, what it considers real for you—and that is the present. This is where you take action which is the most important element in exercising your freedom.[126]

Nietzsche advocated the importance of learning to forget. He would advise you to forget your past and focus on your present instead. In the context of numerous choices, Nietzsche believed your past should not influence your decisions. You should face your opportunities with fresh eyes, unswayed by your past experiences. Similarly, you should avoid letting your decisions be influenced by others. If you do this, Nietzsche suggests, it will give you the courage to make your own choices. He explains:

---

125   Camus, A. (1989). *The Stranger.*

126   Gosetti-Ferencei, J. (2021). *On Being and Becoming: An Existentialist Approach to Life An Existentialist Approach to Life.*

"But even if the future leaves us nothing to hope
for, the wonderful fact of our existing at this present
moment of time gives us the greatest encouragement
to live after our own rule and measure"[127]

Sartre takes the understanding of our past a step further, believing that one should not assign any value to their past at all. This perspective is evident in his work "Nausea" from 1938, where he explains:

"The true nature of the present revealed itself:
it was what exists, and all that was not present
did not exist."[128]

You can indeed learn from your past, but life takes place in the present, as the philosophy explains. This applies to both yourself and how you view others. You should engage with your inner self, your surroundings, and others by being present in the moment. Ultimately, this is the best way to appreciate your opportunities, enabling you to live the life you want and create the future you desire. As Camus describes it in one of his notebooks:

"A real generosity toward the future consists in giving
all to the present"[129]

According to existentialist philosophy, you should ask yourself: what can I change? Instead of focusing on what you cannot change, shift your attention to what you can. An existentialist approach to life requires you to take action, as without it, your freedom never materializes into anything concrete. You may have numerous privileges and an excessive number of opportunities that can im-

---

127   Nietzsche, F. W. (2018). *Schopenhauer as Educator.*

128   Sartre, J. (2013). *Nausea.*

129   Camus, A. (2010). *Notebooks, 1935-1942.*

prove your life, but without action, they will never be realized. In the present, you create a focus on what you can change and what you already have, leading to a greater presence and associated with more joy in life. As the philosopher Simone de Beauvoir describes it:

> "Change your life today. Don't gamble on the future, act now, without delay."[130]

Minimize your alternatives

Our fear of missing out can be reflected in our consumption patterns. We prefer to keep our options open as long as possible.

Let's consider an example unrelated to our consumption pattern: marriage. How would you feel if you were told that you could never divorce your partner? Once you were married, there was no possibility of changing that. You would have to remain married for the rest of your lives.

Such a thought might scare many today, but it was not many years ago when it was not possible to dissolve a marriage. In Denmark, it was only in 1925 that divorce became legal. Before that, leaving a spouse could have been a death sentence, which is why, funnily enough, not many did it. Today, however, the picture is different. Fast forward to 2020, and 48% of marriages ended in divorce in Denmark. And in 2014, the number was over 54%. Today, we have the option to change our decision, thanks to new legislation in most Westernized countries, which we also choose to do, even when it comes to a subject like marriage.[131] [132]

It makes sense that we should not stay in a relationship that is bad for us. But if we put on our "consumer behavior glasses" and

---

130   Beauvoir, S. (1984). *After The Second Sex: Conversations with Simone DeBeauvoir,.*

131   *https://danmarkshistorien.dk/vis/materiale/aegteskabsloven-1922/*

132   *https://www.dst.dk/da/Statistik/emner/borgere/husstande-familier-og-boern/skilsmisser*

see how it affects the way we handle our options, it can present a challenge. Why? Because we keep our options open, which makes us think about our alternatives. This is not just true for our marriages, but in all the decisions we make.

There are other examples of the effect of our alternatives. How would you feel, for example, about signing up for a social event if you were told you could in no way cancel later? In that case, you would not have the option to change your decision if a better alternative arose or if you suddenly realized you actually did not want to participate.

Without any alternatives, our options seem to have a lower value when presented to us. This actually makes sense if we, once again, put on our "consumer behavior glasses." Here, your lack of alternatives automatically leads you to devalue your options. Interestingly, this holds true regardless of how much you want to marry your partner or attend a social event. The only barrier that causes you to devalue your options is your lack of alternatives.

Keeping our options open affects our ability to make decisions as well as our ability to focus on the present. The reason lies in our consumer behavior, where we prefer the possibility of changing our choices. But the availability of alternatives also leads many of us to actually change our choices. The number of divorces can indicate a trend in this direction, although the topic is obviously more complex than that.

The opportunity to change our decision leads us to consider the alternatives at our disposal. But this only occurs when we have the opportunity to think about them. If alternatives did not exist, we would not consider them, and therefore they would not affect our decisions. It may seem restrictive that you have to buy clothes without the option to change your mind and return them free-of-charge. However, it can also be beneficial to avoid too many alternatives in your life, as they focus on everything you do not have, i.e., everything else you could obtain.

Existential philosophy tells us that you only derive value from your actions when you assign them value. Your actions can only contribute to your happiness if you tell yourself they do. If you constantly think there is an alternative to what you are doing, it will rob your choice of its value. Your options become a source of worry because they make you believe you are missing out on something.

It is deeply ingrained in us as humans to want the best of everything, and to believe the grass is always greener on the other side, as the saying goes. And who knows, maybe it is?

But here, philosophy would tell you that the pursuit of perfection and the search for alternatives that might slightly improve your choice is not worth it. The time you spend, both mentally and physically, searching for alternatives is also time you take away from the present. The calculation is therefore in your favor if you focus on the present instead. When you tell yourself there are no alternatives, your only option is to immerse yourself in the choice you have made. Whether it is a social event, a pair of new pants, or the person you choose to share your life with. If you constantly believe that something else could be better, you will eventually come to believe there is something better to pursue. This leads to a loss of what exists in the present.

"Good enough" is the new perfect

As seen in the last section, a lack of alternatives can lead us to immerse ourselves more in the present because it removes the possibility of thinking about what else we could be doing. According to consumer behavior research, we can achieve greater joy from our choices if we convince ourselves that our decisions are good enough. Instead of chasing perfection, Herbert Simon showed with his term 'satisficing' that we can benefit from choosing the first thing that seems good enough. This can save us the mental energy we would spend thinking about our alternatives and actually make us happier.

As a response to our need to shift focus away from the present, Nietzsche presented the Latin term *amor fati*. Translated into English, it means "a love of fate." Nietzsche himself describes it with the words:

> "My formula for human greatness is amor fati: that one wants nothing to be different, not in the future, not in the past, not for all eternity. Not only to endure what is necessary, still less to conceal it—all idealism is falseness in the face of necessity—but to love it..."[133]

There is strength in immersing yourself in the present, by telling yourself that you wish nothing to be different: that everything right now—exactly as it is—is actually perfect. Nietzsche himself explained how he applied this approach to his life, aspiring to be a yes-sayer.

This means being a person who pays attention to the small details like waking up in a bed, being able to pour a cup of coffee, and actually having a roof over your head. Things that no longer drive our thoughts, as they are more focused on choices that allow us to realize ourselves.

Perhaps you know the feeling of having watched a really good movie without any expectations beforehand? Because you did not assign any expectations to the action, it likely seemed exceptionally good. Conversely, you might have also tried watching a new movie that everyone told you was the best ever. But after watching it, you felt it did not live up to your expectations. Had you not heard about the movie before, you likely would not have formed any

---

133   Nietzsche, F. W. (1974). *The Gay Science: With a Prelude in Rhymes and an Appendix of Songs.*

expectations, and you probably would have enjoyed it more. Your expectations thus became a hindrance to enjoying the movie's full value.

Your expectations can lead you to look towards your alternatives. Meanwhile, you remove focus from the present; as in this case, by sitting and thinking about anything else other than enjoying the movie you went to the cinema to see.

Unfortunately, it is not just a trip to the cinema where your expectations can be a hindrance to enjoying the choice you have made. In fact, it can affect all the choices you make, if you set too high expectations. And as you have to make more choices, because the number of your options increases, you can catch yourself thinking that nothing is good. Nietzsche would probably tell you that you should choose to enjoy the movie and love everything that happens right in front of you—everything you get to experience. *Amor fati!*

A workout in decision-making

According to a consumer study, the average couple spends 150 minutes per week deciding what to eat.[134] This adds up to 130 hours a year. Another study reveals that, on average, individuals spend 90-150 minutes each week choosing their outfits, equating to 78-130 hours annually. Additionally, it is found that on average, 50 minutes per week are spent deciding on a movie to watch on Netflix.[135] This means that you spend 43 hours a year finding the perfect movie on Netflix.

Of course, we need to find the right thing to eat, dress as we wish, and watch the movie we prefer. But spending 45 minutes a day making these decisions is unlikely to bring us closer to a higher

---

134   New York Post (2017). *American couples spend 5.5 days a year deciding what to eat.*

135   Castillo, M. (2016). *Younger cord-cutters actually watch TV differently than cable subscribers.*

meaning of life. The above studies are also mentioned in Annie Duke's book "How to Decide" (2020). Here she explains, that...

we, as humans, are gradually becoming pacified, as our options increase.

There are simply so many things to choose from that we need to train ourselves in decision-making. Our ability to do so must be strengthened and maintained if we do not want to become passive and unable to make our own decisions without first assessing all our options.

I believe the root of the problem lies in our mentality that there is always something better. The question is, can we continue like this? The number of our options is increasing, and so are psychological illnesses, such as anxiety. To avoid pacifying ourselves, we must get better at navigating our options. Both in the way we handle our options and in how we relate to the number of them.

One thing is to look at how we handle our options, but we should also look at how we limit them. When faced with a choice, you can try asking yourself: "If this was the only option, would I be satisfied with it?" If the answer is yes, then you can proceed with that option. All our options can be confusing because we want a right answer that may not exist. Here we can lean on the words of Søren Kierkegaard, who in his book "Enten—Eller" (Either/Or) from 1843 writes the famous words:

> "Marry, and you will regret it; don't marry,
> you will also regret it; marry or don't marry,
> you will regret both."[136]

---

136 Translated from old Danish written language "Gift Dig, Du vil fortryde det; gift Dig ikke, Du vil ogsaa fortryde det; gift Dig eller gift Dig ikke, Du vil fortryde begge Dele;" in the book Kierkegaard, S. (2016). *Enten—Eller. Første del.*

His point: There is no right or wrong decision. There is only the decision that you make. Thus, we can make life easier for ourselves by taking action rather than exploring all options.

6. Perspective: The art of failing

What should we do when faced with multiple choices and simultaneously do not want to make the wrong one? As explained, we seem to have created a need to make more choices and execute them all to perfection. We acknowledge that more choices also imply more decisions. However, we forget that the number of our choices and options also affects the number of our mistakes. From an external perspective, it makes sense: more choices imply a greater risk of mistakes. Should not it then be okay to fail? Our need for perfectionism tells a different story, making us view our mistakes negatively. And a fear of failing, combined with more choices and a need for perfectionism, is a dangerous cocktail. A cocktail that can have serious consequences for our mental well-being.

So, how do you avoid it? As you will read in the following, the answer is not to prevent ourselves from making mistakes. On the contrary. We can instead benefit from learning to think about what we dislike rather than what we like. We can also learn that we will make mistakes. We can even manage to make failing an art.

Let's start with an example of how we can focus on what we like and why it makes it harder for us. Maybe you have had to introduce yourself to new people and tell them who you are? Or perhaps you have met someone who immediately asked you, "So, what do you like to do?". The question can be hard to answer because you focus on giving an answer that tells what you enjoy. But your options are nearly endless. You may like many different things, and you might want to watch many different movies. So, what do you do now? You may, like many others—including myself—quickly answer that you like spending time with friends, engage in some form of exercise, and travel now and then. Basically, a non-personal answer that does not necessarily require you to reflect and think about your answer.

The same applies when you are at home and your partner asks (Yes, sorry, here it comes again!): "What would you like to watch on Netflix?". As we have read, we can spend up to 50 minutes a week choosing a movie, so you might well answer: "I don't mind. You choose!". Your brain assesses that there are too many options, so you place the responsibility on your partner to choose the movie.

Fortunately, there is a counter-response that does not require you to say what you like. On the contrary, it is about answering what you do not like. It is relatively simple, but it has a significant impact on how you handle your options. Instead of seeing them as unlimited, you can narrow them down and, in the process, also think about what you like. Back to the Netflix example. You might not know what you want to watch, but at least you know you do not want to watch the same movie you saw last week.

Now, you might be wondering what things you do not like have to do with failing? Well, your brain will try to minimize the number of your options and make them more manageable. This is one of the reasons why our cognitive biases go haywire when our brain feels that you need to make a lot of decisions. In such cases, the brain creates mental shortcuts to narrow down your options, though not always in your favor. However, the idea is sound, as we always try to limit the amount of our options. If we do not, it can seem impossible to give a proper answer.

As humans, we have accustomed ourselves to focus on everything we like. But in a world where our options seem endless, it can be a bit like looking for a needle in a haystack. One thing is how we present ourselves to another person and choose films on Netflix, but it also shows signs of a larger trend affecting our actions. A trend where we avoid thinking about what we do not like—and therefore forget that we also need to learn what we dislike. This can only happen by learning to fail.

All the things you dislike

When you choose to think about everything you like, you can prevent yourself from narrowing down the number of your options. This is particularly evident when you tell yourself that you must make the right choices, and that your choices must be perfect because there is no room for error. But as you can read in this section, it can be beneficial to tell yourself the opposite. Namely, that you will fail, and you will make wrong choices. And as part of this process, you need to accept that you will choose the wrong options and make the wrong decisions. But in the grand scheme of things, this is part of the process of choosing. So, it is not something you can (or should) try to avoid.

**You can explore this mindset by
asking yourself what you do not want,
rather than what you do want.**

This can help you see your options as something to try. Meaning, you do not necessarily need to get it right on the first attempt, and it is okay to miss the mark. At the same time, it helps to narrow down your options while prompting you to reflect on what you really want (by asking yourself what you do not want). As Camus describes in his book "The Stranger":

"I may not have been sure about what really
did interest me, but I was absolutely sure about
what didn't."[137]

In the modern world, where the multitude of options can lead to psychological illnesses like anxiety, it may seem like an art to dare to fail. Or rather, to reconcile with the idea that you will make mistakes. Instead of being knocked down when you make a mis-

---

137   Camus, A. (1989). *The Stranger.*

193

take or choose incorrectly, you should tell yourself that you have learned something. Do not tell yourself that you have lost something, as this makes you focus on your alternatives, and the value you think they could have given you. Instead, tell yourself that you have learned something through your choice, making it not a waste.

Failing gives you valuable knowledge about what you dislike. And that is just as valuable as knowing what you do like.

Think of Sartre's student, who had to choose between going to war or taking care of his mother. As Sartre said, there was no right or wrong choice. There was only the choice the student decided to make. The student choosing a field of study can start by narrowing down their options and asking themselves: "What do I not want to do?". Then, they can tell themselves that they need to try things out, which will involve the risk of making mistakes. But there is nothing wrong with that. On the contrary, it is a natural part of the process of choosing.

Mistakes and decisions go hand in hand. As Nietzsche described, humans function in contrasts; there is no good without the bad. A healthy relationship with your options works the same way; there are no good decisions without mistakes. As seen in earlier sections of the book, it can lead to psychological instability when you tell yourself that you must choose correctly, and all your actions must be perfect, while aiming for 'good enough' is actually the best for your mental well-being. It is almost impossible to choose correctly among your many options.

Therefore, ask yourself what you do not want and narrow down to what you might like and therefore should try. Do not see it as if you have to be right on the first try. There is nothing that is right for everyone, but there may be something that seems right for you.

It is good to fail

In studies conducted by psychology professor Gabriele Oettingen (2014), she examines how it can actually be beneficial to imagine that you will fail. Her research shows the impact of our expectations and how both positive and negative thoughts can influence our ability to realize our goals.

In one of her weight loss studies, she showed that participants who imagined they could not lose weight actually lost more weight on average. Conversely, the study showed that test subjects who imagined it would be easy to achieve their goals did not reach their goals. The latter group did not think they could fail and set high expectations for themselves, resulting in less weight loss than the first group.

Oettingen has conducted research on failure in the context of school, work, and even our ability to recover after surgeries. All her research shows that

**although it does not feel good to imagine that
one will fail, it actually increases the chances of
achieving one's goals.**

In the consulting world, the concept of a 'premortem' is used. This involves thinking about why a given project will fail, even before the project has even started. This exercise is used to avoid potential detours on the way to making the project a success.

You do not need to imagine all scenarios three months into the future or start picking apart every idea as soon as it arises. But you should see that your ability to fail can have many positive aspects. It can actually be advantageous just to think about why and how you will fail. Removing your fear of failure can help you to act and seize the opportunities you are presented with, knowing that many of your choices will lead to mistakes. If you become afraid to make choices because you might make mistakes, you also stop yourself from acting. If you were to be in accordance with the existentialist movement, this is tantamount to renouncing your freedom and thereby the very meaning of life. So, make yourself a world champion in failing, so you can learn what you dislike—and thereby what you do like.

7. Perspective: Make death your ally

The contemplation of death brings about a special reflection on the choices we have made. It is nature's perspective on our actions, compelling us to consider whether we are living the life we desire. Death does not need to be something we fear or ignore until we are face to face with it.

In relation to your choices, pondering death can be helpful if you have lost perspective on your actions. Asking yourself: if you knew you were going to die in a few years, would you prioritize your choices the same way? Or might you choose something entirely different? In such cases, death can even become your ally, providing a wake-up call that prompts you to reflect on the choices you prioritize and, by extension, those you de-prioritize.

Utilizing death

Throughout history, various societies have cultivated their relationship with death and utilized it in multiple ways. When the Greek historian Herodotus visited ancient Egypt, he noted how it was customary to present skeletons to guests after a grand feast (a stark reminder of death indeed). For them, it was a way of appreciating what they had enjoyed and been given. Now, it is not suggested that you distribute skeletons at your next dinner party, but perhaps there is something to learn from incorporating death into our mindset (at least in a less dramatic fashion). We can start by accepting that death is inevitable and that trying to suppress or deny it is useless. As the words of existential philosopher, Martin Heidegger, are used to describe death:

"If I take death into my life, acknowledge it, and face
it squarely, I will free myself from the anxiety of death
and the pettiness of life—and only then will I be free
to become myself."[138]

When you think of death as something inevitable, it can help
to view your actions from a broader perspective. As Heidegger
ideas sound, it can help to shift focus away from 'the pettiness of
life.' Thus, death can prompt you to think about what truly matters. In our pursuit to achieve as much as possible, we also aspire to
realize as many of life's opportunities as we can. We may find ourselves thinking that everything must happen faster, and that more
is always better. However, as Camus explains, we should remember
that each day brings us closer to death:

"We build our life on the hope for tomorrow, yet
tomorrow brings us closer to death and we forget that
we do die one day."[139]

Existential philosophy does not believe that we should forget
that death is a part of living. On the contrary, it argues that we
should confront death, after which it can serve as a powerful tool
enabling us to make authentic decisions. If we do not consider
death, we are deceiving ourselves. Acknowledging that life has an
end is beneficial, according to existential thought. By viewing life
as endless, we impose no limitations on ourselves. Therefore, when
navigating our options, we also fail to see any limitations. Death
is a necessary boundary that prompts you to ask yourself: "Is this
really what I want to spend my time on?"

---

138   Described in the works of Lavine (1985). *From Socrates to Sartre: The Philosophic
Quest* (New York: Bantam, 1985), p. 332

139   Camus, A. (2018). *The Myth of Sisyphus.*

Opportunity to choose

I have now presented the seven perspectives from existential philosophy, each focusing on how we handle our options. In the following section, these various perspectives are brought together and related to the paradox of plenty. We can start by asking ourselves whether we have forgotten that our options are just that—options? In the face of an increasing number of options, have we made them out to be more than they are? And have we forgotten that we do not need to act on most of them, but that we actually have a choice?

As mentioned, it appears that as the number of options increases, so does the occurrences of mental illnesses. This is particularly true of illnesses like anxiety, which are associated with having to make more decisions.

Our options, therefore, seem to come with a mental burden.

But according to existential philosophy, there is no right and wrong. There is only the joy that you assign to your own choices. And there are only bad and wrong decisions if you tell yourself that they are.

The philosophy tells us that our options have value, but that value is only realized when we take action. Therefore, we can appropriately tell ourselves that we have the opportunity to choose. And this is not the same as saying that we must choose. Or as the quote from Sartre goes:

"It isn't freedom from. It's freedom to."[140]

He emphasizes that you should view your freedom as something that enables you to decide to do something. You should enjoy your options, rather than feeling trapped by them. A good starting point for this is to reduce their number.

---

140   "It isn't freedom from. It's freedom to." by Jean-Paul Sartre

Reduce the number of options

Choosing requires energy, and in a world with many options, it can drain your mental surplus. Research in consumer behavior refers to this as decision fatigue, and as mentioned, it can lead to thoughtless actions. As a result, your routines and habits may take over, while you find yourself comparing yourself with others. Both of these remove focus from the present moment and from yourself, which existential philosophy associates with living an inauthentic life. Instead, you should make decisions about your options.

Even when you tell yourself that you do not want to choose, you are still making a choice. You cannot avoid it, but you can try to minimize the number of things you have to decide on. The alternative is that your options can feel overwhelming, which can paralyze your ability to make a decision. Or, as consumer behavior describes, your many choices can lead to analysis paralysis. Especially if you try to analyze your way to the perfect decision (which, as explained, does not exist according to existential philosophy).

> **You can reduce the number of your options through the following considerations:**
>
> **Tell yourself that there is no right and wrong:** There is only what you choose. Do as Herbert Simon did and be satisfied with your choice being good enough. This minimizes the number of your options, making it easier to choose among them. Instead of analyzing and considering all possible options you can think of, opt for the first one that reasonably satisfies your needs. You can tell yourself that a good life is filled with mediocre food and decent movies on Netflix.[141]

---

141   Simon, H. A. (1947). *Administrative Behavior: A Study of Decision Making Processes in Administrative Organization.*

Keep focus on yourself and your own choices: Look at the options you have in front of you and do not look at others, as you are most likely to compare yourself with them (which will only lead to even more options). Instead, keep focus on yourself, and when the thought arises telling you that something better exists, you can aptly ask yourself: "If I stuck with my current decision—and there were no other options—would I be satisfied?". If the answer is yes, then it means your choice is good enough. And good enough is actually really good when we talk about mental well-being and many options.

Limit what you have to decide on: We know it can take a long time to decide simple things like clothing choice or what to eat. You can choose to give yourself only a limited number of options. It could be that you only have a few sets of clothes that you wear, or a handful of restaurants from which you order take-away. How you put it together is up to you. Several well-known people like Bill Gates, Vera Wang, and Mark Zuckerberg (and many more) tell us that they have a daily "uniform" they put on. This way they avoid spending time and mental energy deciding what clothes to wear. The same mentality can be applied in life to avoid spending time on decisions you do not want to spend time on.

Engage in the present: Remove possibilities of thinking about everything else you could be doing. Focus on the present and do not let your mind wander too much. A wandering mind causes you to devalue what you are doing and therefore the things you already have. A lack of focus on the present also brings forth more options that you think you need to consider. Meanwhile, it provokes a need to have more and more.

> **Don't cry over missed opportunities:** Have you missed an opportunity? Then tell yourself that it is good to miss out on something. It means you are giving yourself the opportunity to focus on the present and yourself. Believing that you are always missing out on something can make you think that something better is always waiting out there.

Tell your own story

A key characteristic of a difficult decision is that you cannot separate the opportunity from its alternatives. Unlike an easy decision, where you can quickly see that one alternative is better than the others.[142]

When we cannot judge or comprehend what is best, we tend to choose the safe option. However, the safe choice is not always the best, as it may be influenced by decision fatigue, analysis paralysis, cognitive biases, and many other terms discussed in this book. Your brain has plenty of shortcuts to make it easier to make choices. But making it easier for you to choose still means making decisions where you consider yourself and remain authentic.

So, how do you remain authentic and assign value to your choices? You can create your own narrative and story associated with your choices. You can create the meaning and reason behind the choices you make. You can make it easier for yourself to choose if you also tell yourself that it is the right choice. Assure yourself that you support your own decision. Instead of relying on others' approval, prioritize your own acceptance of them. In doing so, you can better stand by your choices and the opportunities you seize.

In unfolding your own story—through your choices—existential philosophy suggests that you should be willing to explore the unknown. Create an existence where you do not form a distrust of your reality, but remain down-to-earth by telling yourself that your reality is the only reality. In other words, your existence can only

---

142   Chang, R. (2015). *Transformative Choices.*

be perceived subjectively. Therefore, do not succumb to the belief that there is an objective truth. If you do, the philosophy explains, you are not dealing with your life, but rather with a utopian understanding that other people know something you do not.

A maze of opportunities without an objective answer

Searching for a predetermined meaning in life does not bring us closer to happiness. We may chase things that gain acceptance and status among others, but ultimately, philosophy tells us that we must acknowledge the hard truth: there is no objective answer.

Balancing a life where you try to avoid failure and follow what others tell you is good does not necessarily lead to something good for you. On the contrary, you might end up focusing all your time on balancing your options while forgetting to enjoy them. Avoiding this requires an understanding of the impact that the paradox of choice can have on you. It is essential for changing the way you see your options as something positive. Otherwise, they can even become a mental burden.

Regardless of where we are from or what we try to achieve through life's many options, we all have a responsibility to open ourselves to what our options can offer us. This does not mean we should view life as something absurd or our happiness as something unattainable. Instead, we should see the abundance of our options as a maze that requires us to make mistakes and go wrong, but ultimately leads us to an authentic life based on actions we ourselves choose to take. Our options make it possible, but first, we must dare to explore them. If we can do that, we also achieve the freedom that our options contain but do not always deliver on their own. As we begin to explore the opportunities that differ from our common understanding of what we think we should do, our anxiety begins to subside as the complex beauty of our choices reveals itself.

There is no objective answer or a 10-step guide that can ensure you will be happy. Yet, you can help create the necessary perspectives for yourself and your actions, which can set you on the right course. Your right course is your own and thus not driven by others' thoughts on what they consider meaningful.

SISYPHUS SMILED
UP THE MOUNTAIN

A world that offers more than ever before also demands more from us. Or at least, that is what we tell ourselves. Studies from the world of psychology and consumer behavior show that we struggle to navigate among our options: that something good, created on the basis of our freedom and welfare, can actually have a negative effect.

As you have read, it is estimated that up to one in three people will suffer from a mental illness at some point in their life in a wealthy Westernized country such as Denmark: a country that has been ranked on of the happiest countries in the world.

And because the way we handle our options is connected to mental illnesses—such as anxiety and depression—it is not a subject we should ignore. On the contrary, it is something we need to learn to deal with. For instance, through the existentialist perspectives presented in this book. We cannot expect the number of our options to decrease significantly in the near future. Thus, it is up to us to learn to navigate among them.

Our choices—and life in general—can sometimes feel absurd. But we are not given the good in life without also receiving the bad. Here, existentialist philosophy tells us that the good in life is connected to the difficult. Or as Camus writes in his book "The Myth of Sisyphus" (1942):

"Happiness and the absurd are two sons of the same earth. They are inseparable. It would be a mistake to say that happiness necessarily springs from the absurd discovery. It happens as well that the feeling of the absurd springs from happiness."

Existential philosophy can help us focus on our own values. In a world where our options lead us to do the opposite, philosophy can seem like a friend in disguise. Existential thoughts may seem radical to some, while for others they may seem like a healthy reality check. When the world works against us, and our actions lack meaning, we can lean on its perspectives. Sometimes what seems radical and different at first glance turns out to be a necessity.

Sisyphus was condemned to roll a stone up a mountain for all eternity. Only when he realized that there was nothing more to his life than rolling a stone up the mountain did he find meaning in his actions. He acknowledged that it was his life, so it was no use fleeing from his fate, only embracing it. It may have seemed absurd, but he still managed to find meaning. He chose not to focus on other people, but on himself, because he knew that meaning had to be created in the present and through his own actions—no one else could create it for him.

So do not imagine Sisyphus complaining his way up the mountain. Instead, imagine him smiling as he pushed his stone. He learned to find meaning in his actions and united himself with his choices, even under the most difficult conditions. Can the rest of us learn the same?

Camus concludes his story with the words:

"The struggle itself towards the heights is enough to fill a man's heart. One must imagine Sisyphus happy."[143]

---

143   *"The Myth of Sisyphus"* (1942)

www.ingramcontent.com/pod-product-compliance
Lightning Source LLC
LaVergne TN
LVHW011009200726

843509LV00011B/1030